THE UNIVERSITY OF MICHIGAN
CENTER FOR JAPANESE STUDIES

MICHIGAN PAPERS IN JAPANESE STUDIES
NO. 3

THE JAPANESE AUTOMOTIVE INDUSTRY:
MODEL AND CHALLENGE FOR THE FUTURE?


Edited by

Robert E. Cole


Ann Arbor

Center for Japanese Studies
The University of Michigan

1981

*Open access edition funded by the National Endowment for the Humanities/
Andrew W. Mellon Foundation Humanities Open Book Program.*

Library of Congress Cataloging in Publication Data

Main entry under title:

The Japanese automotive industry.

(Michigan papers in Japanese studies: no. 3)

    1. Automobile industry and trade—Japan—Addresses, essays,
lectures. I. Cole, Robert E. II. University of Michigan. Center
for Japanese studies. III. Series.
HD9710.J32J37          338.4'76292'0952         81-6185
ISBN 978-0-939512-08-9 (pbk)        AACR2

Printed and bound by CPI Group (UK) Ltd, Croydon, CR0 4YY

ISBN 978-0-939512-08-9 (paper)
ISBN 978-0-472-88004-1 (ebook)
ISBN 978-0-472-90203-3 (open access)

# TABLE OF CONTENTS

TABLE OF CONTENTS, continued

## Preface

As those of us at the Center for Japanese Studies reflected on the deteriorating position of the domestic auto industry in the fall of 1980, and the strong competitive threat being posed by the Japanese automakers, we were struck by the extraordinarily low quality of the public discussion of these critical issues. The national importance of the issues seemed only matched by the superficiality of the analyses being offered. The tendency to think in terms of scapegoats was particularly evident. The Japanese as the basic cause of our problems has been a particularly notable theme. To be sure, cooperation with the Japanese in formulating a rational overall trade policy may be an important part of the solution. It has also been fashionable to blame it all on American auto industry management for not concentrating on the production of small cars when "everyone knew" that was the thing to do. Alternatively, government meddling was blamed for all our problems. Clearly, the complex problem we faced required more penetrating analyses. It seemed to us therefore that the time was ripe for a public seminar which moved beyond the rhetoric of the moment and probed some of the deeper causes of our problems and possible directions for future policy.

Consider the increase in unemployment among auto workers which has provoked much of the growing public sentiment in America to take political action. To attribute this unemployment simply to the Japanese market penetration, or to the derelictions of our own industry and workers, or to misguided government policies confesses some ignorance of current market conditions and production developments affecting present and future employment opportunities in the domestic auto industry. The internationalization of the auto market, the industry's trend toward worldwide sourcing, growing automation, and the shift to smaller cars which use less materials all presage a sizeable permanent reduction of the labor force employed to produce cars. These processes operate for the most part independent of Japanese market penetration. To give a sense of the magnitude of these developments, according to one industry projection, by 1985 we will be sourcing 25 percent (in dollar value) of auto components outside of the United States.

Moreover, much of the impact of unemployment will be concentrated in the five major auto states: Michigan, Ohio, Indiana, New York, and Illinois. The movement toward lighter materials such as aluminum as well as the increasing emphasis on electronics all create employment opportunities outside the industry's traditional midwestern heartland; the reduction in use of such materials as cast iron will dramatically reduce employment in the midwestern foundries. Proposed accelerated depreciation schedules for capital investment and other tax policies as well as expected increases in new plant investment also encourage geographical diversification. Outmigration from the affected region will surely occur, but unemployment and its attendant misfortunes will still be severe and may be ameliorated only by major efforts. There is no guarantee of federal relief, and no guarantee that even if such relief were available needed basic adjustments would quickly occur. Some state treasuries are presently hardpressed, Michigan's among them.

In holding the January 1981 auto conference, we took it as our task to begin addressing the critical issues facing the industry, with particular, but not exclusive, attention to examining the role of the Japanese auto industry. We had in mind not simply to conduct a rational discussion of the trade issue but to probe the sources of Japanese competitive strength, especially those features whose study might profit us.

Americans have not had very good access to information on Japanese industry, an ignorance imposed principally by the cultural and language barrier between the two countries. Some rather simplistic formulations of the sources of Japanese strength and the lessons to be learned having gained currency on both sides of the Pacific, a serious dialogue on the central issues appeared timely. Reflecting on the public seminar and the articles presented in this volume, we can hardly be satisfied with our success. In some respects, we may even have contributed to establishing some new myths. Nevertheless, critical issues were explored and important information presented. Much remains to be done; by the Center for Japanese Studies and the University of Michigan, for one, in nurturing what useful and clearly needed beginnings were made.

I would like to thank Harold Shapiro, President of the University, for his strong support for the plan to hold the seminar, and David Cole, Director of the Office for the Study of Automotive Transportation, Donald Smith, Director of the Industrial Development Division, and Al Sussman, Dean of the Rackham School of Graduate Studies, who served with me on the planning committee. David Stark performed heroically as conference coordinator. Numerous others gave unstintingly of their time and expertise.

Those who attended the public seminar can testify to the almost electric atmosphere throughout the day. The strong need for good information upon which to base policy was apparent. The seminar received national attention in the analyses of such respected journals as Ward's Automotive Report and Science.

In these proceedings, we bring those discussions to a wider audience. Question and answer sessions at the conference were necessarily short and a few speakers delivered abbreviated remarks; this volume restores a number of omissions, and provides additional answers to some pertinent questions put by our audience. We hope to encourage the serious problem-solving these complex issues demand. Far too much time has been spent trying to fix the blame.

Robert E. Cole
Director
Center for Japanese Studies

# INTRODUCTORY REMARKS TO THE CONFERENCE

## Harold T. Shapiro

It is a pleasure to welcome you all to the University of Michigan and to this important conference. I would like to extend a special welcome to today's speakers and, in particular, to Secretary of Transportation Neil E. Goldschmidt and to Senators Carl M. Levin and Donald W. Riegle, Jr. Their presence here today bears witness to their deep concern regarding the matters before us today, and to their commitment, both to the State of Michigan and to the restructuring and reinvigoration of the national economy. I would also like to thank my colleagues here at the University of Michigan who, by serving on the planning committee, have managed to bring an initial idea regarding the conference to its fruition here today. The timeliness of the discussions that we will hear today is borne witness to by the extraordinary public interest in this conference and an actual attendance far in excess of what we had anticipated.

We at the University of Michigan are particularly glad to have played a part in organizing this conference and in hosting it here on the Ann Arbor campus. We are pleased because we will be addressing a series of challenges that are important, relevant, and challenging. It is clear that simple, old solutions are just not adequate to meet the complex set of issues on which our discussions will focus today. It is also true, of course, that the future of the automotive industry here in the United States has a special importance and urgency to the State of Michigan. The University of Michigan, therefore, is pleased to have been able to use this opportunity to offer some leadership in helping ourselves, the nation, and the industrial community around the world in seriously discussing the chal-

1

lenges that are before us. I hope the conference will result in elevating the level of national and international discussions on these issues.

I would like to comment briefly on the broad context of today's discussion. It seems to me that the most critical thing for us all to realize is that the world economy is going through a dramatic transformation. Perhaps the most important aspect of this transformation is a growing interdependence of all industrial and, indeed, non-industrial economies. Trade growth in the last three decades has run far ahead of expectations and forecasts. This growing interdependence of world economies contains within it both great gains and great challenges. One of the implications of this growing interdependence is a redistribution of production between the key economies of the world. At the same time, however, this redistribution is accompanied by difficult transitions, especially for the mature economies of Western Europe and North America. Although the change in the global economic order is positive, we must at the same time face up to the challenges presented within those industrial sectors and particular geographic locations which must go through difficult transition periods.

This is especially true for the economies of Western Europe and North America which face two additional factors, the emergence of new competitors (such as Japan) and the energy crisis, which demand yet a further restructuring of existing economic structures and relationships. This restructuring and shifting is for our mutual benefit, the mutual benefit of all the world economies, but the transition must still be managed and managed carefully. This is one of our major challenges.

Further, all these changing forces on the economic side are accompanied by an equally important set of changes in our social lives. Our expectations and our general attitudes toward our society are changing dramatically. This is true of our attitudes toward work, government, family, church, trade unions, corporations, etc. The list covers most major institutions in society.

All of these forces are clearly recognizable in the automotive industry, especially here in the State of Michigan, the home of automotive production. Thus, in a particularly concentrated form your discussions deal with an important and critical, but rather typical problem in today's changing world economy. The benefits of this discussion can flow beyond the automotive industry and help us confront similar challenges throughout the world economy.

In closing, I would like to consider two particular things highlighted by the title of this conference. The title, "The Japanese Automotive Industry: Model and Challenge for the Future?" highlights two particular things. It highlights the Japanese automotive industry. We focus attention here not because the Japanese have done something undesirable or bad, but because they may have done something well, and we ought to discuss what we have to learn from their experience. More important, however, is the question mark which appears at the end of the title. This perhaps is the most significant aspect of the title itself and it signifies in my mind that we are engaged in an ongoing discussion and not stating a series of conclusions. That is the purpose of this conference and I hope the discussions are conducted in this light.

Once again, it is a great pleasure for the University of Michigan to welcome you all here and we wish all participants in the conference success with today's discussion.

# THE GOVERNMENT, BUSINESS, AND LABOR PERSPECTIVE

Paul W. McCracken

Not since the years of the Great Depression, now almost a half-century ago, have the fortunes of a major U.S. industry shifted so abruptly from the viable to the ominous as in the case of today's U.S. automobile companies. Executives of the smallest of the four are now presumably learning to speak French, Chrysler has survived into 1981 through transfusions from the Federal Treasury, the two largest companies are experiencing hemorrhaging losses, and Michigan's unemployment rate is now the highest in the nation.

This does not, of course, mean that the whole U.S. economy is thereby threatened with extinction. Auto GNP, that part of our total output of goods and services accounted for by this industry, is normally only 3 1/2 percent of the whole economy. While each industry, education by no means excluded, considers itself to be peculiarly strategic and with an importance for the economy far transcending its own industry boundary lines, recent developments in the North American auto industry are a source of concern not only in this country but internationally.

Some key questions are now being asked, and asked with growing urgency. How these questions are answered will influence the directions of policy for years to come. First, are our problems simply another case of an industry which misread the omens of change in the economy, or is incapable of adapting to progress, and therefore one that should go the way of, for example, those making steam locomotives or horse-drawn buggies? If so, painful as the results would be for those adversely affected, it would not be a

5

particularly unique case in economic history. Economic progress has always consisted of displacing the old with the new, and for those in industries thus dis-established the process has always been painful. The chairman of my own doctoral committee years ago, J. A. Schumpeter, summed it up with a pregnant chapter title, "The Process of Creative Destruction." Some in the industry have themselves intimated that they did not perceive quickly enough the portents of change.

A second question has to do with how much of our problems originated in government policies. These government policies themselves have seemed often to be giving conflicting signals. Requirements for reducing gasoline consumption per mile were established, and government then resolutely lured people toward larger cars by holding gasoline prices below world levels. Indeed, as recently as two years ago it was inventories of small cars that were uncomfortably heavy.

Third, is the problem that costs are simply too high in the U.S. industry. There is at least enough circumstantial evidence to suggest that this question must be raised. Perhaps adverse cost differentials were until recently masked by the preference here for large cars. American companies were thus somewhat insulated from industries abroad whose domestic markets made tooling up for large cars uneconomic. The sudden shift of American motorists toward smaller cars about two years ago, precipitated by the advent of gasoline lines, then removed this insulation, exposing our industry to the full force of foreign competition.

Finally, has Japan developed some sort of a generalized unfair advantage in the international markets? The number of people in the United States, and even more in Western Europe, answering this question in the affirmative is undoubtedly growing. Different people cite different features of the politico-economic structure there to support this point. National policy seems to have skewed the economy toward a highly developed industrial sector, leaving a costly and often a seemingly impenetrable distribution system that effectively limits imports. Others insist that macro-economic policies of Japan have been oriented toward an artificial stimulation of exports by sustaining an under-valued yen. These policies would range from exchange controls too long retained to a strategy of export-propelled growth—with, as in 1980, a sluggish domestic demand for output retarding imports.

As Mr. Masahiko Ishizuka observed in the Nihon Keizai Shimbun issue of January 6, 1981:

> the year also was characterized by growth largely fueled by external sales, with domestic demand . . . continuing in slump. One inevitable consequence was heightened trade frictions with importing countries.

For both domestic and international reasons it is important for all of us to get a clear-eyed focus on this auto industry problem and on its implications for policy. The questions that must be thought through in arriving at a national policy are formidable. As the American industry settles into a new stability, will its employment base be found permanently to have shrunk? Does government, whose often-conflicting policies contributed to the North American industry's present woes, have an obligation to help the industry regain its equilibrium? If so, what should that assistance be? Can a way be found to enlarge the incomes of the auto workers that would be consistent with re-aligning our costs with international levels? Are we facing permanently high unemployment in auto labor markets? Are there national defense implications in the industry's present condition, or is this the usual national defense argument invoked by a declining domestic industry that is in trouble?

Clearly the present disequilibrium in the auto industry internationally does pose a major threat to the liberal trading and financial order so carefully built up during the last three decades. This liberal order in turn has made a major contribution to rising material levels of living throughout the world. Trade in real terms has expanded at rates almost double that for world GNP (in real terms). And nations for whom trade is particularly important have a particularly important stake in not having this liberal economic order disintegrate. The interwar period taught us that such a disintegration of a liberal economic order, once under way, is not readily reversed.

These are the issues that will constitute the day's agenda. It is a heavy agenda. For that reason introductions will be characterized by a brevity not consistent with the distinction of our speakers.

# THE FUTURE OF THE U.S. AUTO INDUSTRY

## Neil Goldschmidt

It is altogether fitting and proper that my last formal speech as Secretary of Transportation be in this state, to this audience, on this subject.

For the issue of the future health and competitive strength of the U.S. auto industry and its supplier industries has occupied the central place in my administration of the Department—as I believe it will occupy the central place on our nation's agenda over the decade of the 1980s.

Let no one misperceive the vital importance of this matter of the health of our industrial base:

this issue is fundamental;

it is intrinsic to our country's future well-being;

it is essential to our fulfilling the aspirations of our people;

it is crucial to our safeguarding the most basic of our trusts, our national security.

Yesterday, in our nation's capital, I released my report to President Carter on the future of the American auto industry. It came as the culmination of more than a year of hard work; of detailed research and analysis; of visits to assembly plants and steel mills; of conversations with managers, frustrated over the lack of capital available to expand their plants; with workers, frustrated over the lack of jobs in our bread-and-butter industries; with local government officials, frustrated over the lack of resources available to contend with the global changes washing over their communities— and each concerned over the future economic strength of this country. We talked, as well, with the leaders of industry, labor and government of the nations of the world with whom we compete, including the Japanese—and could see their strategies, policies, and programs targeted very clearly and coldly on the objectives of economic growth and employment through trade.

We arrived, after all of this work, at an alarming picture of the decade ahead:

>The shape of the world auto market has been altered permanently and dramatically. No longer is our market distinct from the rest of the world—there is only one auto market—an international one.

>Indeed, this country's market will be the international economic battleground of the 1980s. It is the largest, most accessible market in the world.

>In this life-or-death battle, U.S. automakers are starting from behind. They come late to the production of small, fuel-efficient autos demanded by the market. At a time of record losses, they must make record expenditures to re-tool—while the foreign competition accumulates retained earnings as ammunition for future re-tooling or a price war.

>At the bottom line, our automakers face competition from Japan which appears to hold a $1,000 to $1,500 per vehicle comparative cost advantage based on greater productivity, lower wage rates and more favorable government relations.

>Finally, in spite of—or in some instances because of— our efforts to compete, in the decade ahead we stand to lose permanently roughly one-half a million manufacturing jobs concentrated in a handful of states and cities.

While these conclusions may provide cold comfort to U.S. managers, workers, and government officials, I do not believe this analysis to be overly pessimistic. Indeed the points may be stated even more starkly:

The $1,000 to $1,500 per auto advantage of the Japanese <u>must</u> be met if our industry is to regain its competitive stature in this decade.

Less than one-half—perhaps as little as one-third—of that advantage is attributable to wage rates; the rest must be found in productivity differences and government policies.

It will take a minimum of five years for our industry to meet the challenge from Japan—assuming that we use those five years to good advantage.

From my recent visit to Japan and my conversations there with the leadership in government and industry, I conclude the following: the Japanese do not think that we will use the next five years wisely—I perceive that they judge that this country lacks the will, the <u>guts</u>—to do what is necessary to recapture industrial leadership. They regard us with the cold eye of competition as a one car company country for the future.

<u>If</u> they are right; <u>if</u> our automakers lose more market share; <u>if</u> we fail to meet the competitive challenge from abroad, then our job losses here at home will make the original estimate of half a million seem paltry. Our entire industrial base— steel, iron, rubber, aluminum, and all—will be at peril.

If these judgments sound harsh it is only to sound the alarm and to prod all those concerned—industry, labor, the Congress and new Administration, the American people—to address the critical questions before us:

Can this nation accept a permanent shrinkage of our industrial base?

Can we, rather, design a strategy to interrupt these dangerous trends and return this key industry and our larger industrial base to competitive health?

In my view, the answers to these questions must be self-evident. Not only because of the important role those industries play in providing employment for our people; or simply because of the close relationship between these industries and our energy future.

Transcending these concerns is the issue of our national security. In the past, the production capacity of these basic industries has been a vital mobilizing force in our defense capability. Today, and in the future, we see how important these industries are to defining our might in the world. For as much or more than the power of our arms, it is the power of our industrial economy that establishes our international leadership.

After our recent experience with imported oil, does anyone truly believe that it matters little whether we import growing amounts of basic manufacturing products?

Does anyone believe that it is in our own self-interest to adopt national policies that allow our industrial base to shrink permanently?

Policies that allow basic manufacturing jobs to disappear and critical skills to vanish from our workforce?

Does anyone believe that any of our competitor nations would adopt a set of policies so blind to national self-interest?

I do not believe it.

And I do not believe that that is what Americans want.

Rather, I see the people of this country ready to do what is necessary to re-tool American industry and to re-assert American leadership.

To accomplish that goal, I have recommended to President Carter a new American compact, forged equally among management, labor and government, and based on the following blueprint:

First, government should negotiate an import restraint agreement with the Japanese which reflects the time period it will take for U.S. automakers to accomplish the transition. This would define a reasonable period of time for our domestic industry to re-tool without facing the permanent loss of additional market share. However, the expiration of the agreement would indicate the need for expeditious investments to meet the re-opened competition.

In addition, government should commit to help the industry and its suppliers obtain the capital required to compete. Government may look to undertake general changes in the tax code; or changes specifically targeted on the needs of this industry and its suppliers, or, if necessary, to create an institution such as a re-industrialization finance corporation. The central objective: a signal to the financial sector that this industry will continue to be an attractive place for investment.

For its part, labor should agree to a wage strategy designed to close the differential with Japan.

Management, in return for labor's wage restraint, should be prepared to compensate labor with a negotiated program which could include profit-sharing or other incentives. In this way, organized labor's restraint of today would become a vehicle for future interest in the profitability of the revitalized industry of tomorrow.

In addition to this centerpiece for the compact, I have recommended to the President that:

Government reform its approach to regulation; re-define its antitrust laws; increase support for worker re-training and community re-development; and continue to pursue a shared program of basic research as a joint government-industry responsibility.

Labor continue its support of measures to improve productivity; reduce absenteeism; improve quality; and promote new forms of worker re-training and re-employment.

Management substantially improve productivity; restructure its relationship with labor; intensify research and development; and accept more responsibility for the social and environmental impacts of their products and production facilities, including commitment to build and source in this country.

The key to this report, to these recommendations, and to the whole concept of a compact is its balance.

I do not believe the blame for our nation's industrial dilemma can be laid solely at the door of the temple of labor, or the offices of government, or the executive suite of management. Anyone who believes these critical problems can be solved by slashing at labor, or by cutting at government is worse than mistaken—he is threatening our capacity to find the solution.

For the true solution must be in the efforts of all three—to end the adversarial relationship of the past and to create the cooperative compact our future requires.

There is another danger—that this debate over a great question of our country's future may get cut up into its smallest pieces; that it may be argued at the level of the lowest common denominator.

In my view, that would be a tragedy.

This is not a debate that can be carried by setting the principles of foreign trade versus protectionism; or inflation versus anti-inflation policy; or industrial policy that picks winners and losers versus marketplace economics—and other such pairings and twists.

This is finally a debate which must get us back to basics—to our own self-interest in an international economic competition in which the other nations of the world surely recognize their self-interests, are following those self-interests, and can be expected to continue to follow those self-interests.

It is time we recognized the intrinsic relationship between our industrial power and our national security—not so our companies can parade through the halls of Congress, trumpeting the theme of national security to avoid producing safe autos; not so our unions can salute the banner of national security to avoid the elimination of jobs that block productivity gains.

But so that we can make the adjustments, the sacrifices, the investments needed to improve this country's industrial vigor, retain our manufacturing workforce, and re-develop the cities and towns which have been home to our workers and industries. That, finally, is the vision of America to which we all must bend our efforts.

This nation shared one of the most inspirational moments of last year when a group of hard-fighting, under-dog U.S. hockey players met the challenge of international competition and captured the Olympic gold medal. In their accomplishment this nation felt again the pride and strength of American achievement matched against the best the world could offer.

But remember what it took them to win.

Their coach said it.

"If you want to play this game effectively," Coach Brooks told his players, "you'd better report with a hard hat and lunch pail. If not, you better go watch some old guys ice-fishing."

That is where it stands—in autos, in steel, in world competition.

If we want to play effectively; if we mean business—if we're tired of watching ice-fishing—then it is time for America to report with hard hats and lunch pails.

It is time for all of us to get to work together.

# U.S. - JAPAN TRADE RELATIONS:
## REACHING AN ACCOMMODATION

Yasuhiko Suzuki

Ladies and gentlemen, my name is Yasuhiko Suzuki. I am a vice-president of Nissan Motor Corporation in U.S.A., the sales, marketing, and service subsidiary organization in the United States of Nissan Motor Company, Ltd., Japan—manufacturer of Datsun cars and trucks. I wish to clarify the fact that I am not here today representing the Japanese automobile manufacturers or industry.

It is an honor for me to be here this morning to share this podium with so many distinguished guests from all segments of the automobile industry. I must admit, however, that I am here with some reservation. In fact, coming at this particular time to Michigan, the center of the American auto industry, to discuss the Japanese perspective on our trade relations makes me feel a bit like a member of the cast of your recent television series "Shogun"—only I'm the shipwrecked Englishman and this is the land of the Samurai.

The topic of my contribution to today's proceedings is: "U.S.-Japan Trade Relations: Reaching an Accommodation." As the previous speakers have pointed out, this is a very timely subject given the American industry's concern about its adjustment to new market conditions and, I might add, the Japanese industry's concern about its future in the American market.

I would like to begin by discussing the Japanese perspective on the current auto trade problem between our two countries, and then talk about the type of accommodation that will preserve the vital interests of all.

17

Over the past many months I have listened for <u>many</u> days to testimony comprising thousands of pages on the state of the American auto industry and the role of the Japanese manufacturers. If I were to draw on these various statements to construct the composite view of our trade relations held by many Americans, it would be something like this:

> The monolithic Japanese auto industry, working hand in hand with its government, has brought the American auto industry to its knees with a deliberate flood of imports, frequently sold at unfair prices, while working diligently to keep foreign-made vehicles out of its home market in Japan, and making no contribution whatsoever to the American economy.

If I thought these allegations were true, I don't think I would like us very much either! But the fact is that this is a highly misleading picture of what has happened in our trade relations over the past two years. Let me take apart this hypothetical statement and address each of its five components separately, from the Japanese point of view.

<u>First and foremost</u>, Japanese manufacturers do not believe the current automobile problem in the United States is an issue of imports vs. domestics, but rather a question of small cars vs. large cars. The shortages and rapidly escalating price of gasoline in 1979 caused a fundamental shift in consumer demand from large, fuel-inefficient autos to small, fuel-efficient vehicles. The U.S. International Trade Commission found, for example, that large cars comprised about 50 percent of U.S. apparent consumption from 1975 through 1978, but dropped to about 40 percent in 1979 and to about 30 percent during the first six months of 1980.

Senator Adlai Stevenson on the floor of the Senate on December 12, 1980, clarified this fact, and I quote:

> In addition to the investigation by the International Trade Commission, reports by the Secretary of Transportation, the House Ways and Means Subcommittee on Trade, the Congressional Budget Office and the Council of Economic Advisors—all

conclude that imports are not the source of the U.S.'s difficulties and that import quotas or tariffs would have negligible effects on employment levels although substantial price increases would follow.

Detroit was not prepared for either the quickness or the magnitude of this shift in consumer preference. But already the situation is beginning to correct itself with the American industry's small car capacity <u>increasing</u> from 3.7 million units in 1979 to 5.6 million units in 1981.

The Japanese companies have <u>not</u> flooded the American market, nor are they preparing to do so. Imports have been drawn in to fill the <u>temporary</u> gap between domestic production and consumer demand for small cars. This is not a case of Japanese push, but rather of American pull.

Apart from this change in market demand, at least a portion of the American industry's current problem is caused by adverse economic conditions, including recession, inflation, and high interest rates, all of which have cut the overall level of consumer demand for new automobiles. The difficult state of the U.S. economy has affected import as well as domestic car sales.

<u>Second</u>: as an executive of a Japanese auto company, I can testify that our industry in Japan is neither monolithic nor government-controlled. In fact, Japan has one of the most intensely competitive automotive sectors in the world, with more independent manufacturers than any other industrialized country. In a market less than half the size of the U.S. market, we have nine passenger vehicle producers compared to your five. While these competitive conditions have made us place a premium on product quality and finely sharpen our marketing skills, they have not led to a cartelization of our industry.

<u>Third</u>: and I state this emphatically! Nissan is <u>not</u> engaged in any unfair trade practices in selling its vehicles in the United States, and to my knowledge, neither are any of the other Japanese manufacturers. We are <u>not</u> dumping autos on the American market, nor does the government subsidize our companies.

Fourth: despite the widely held impression in this country, the Japanese auto market is not closed to foreign imports. This may have been true years ago, but it is not true today, for the following reasons:

1) The Japanese government has eliminated all tariffs on imported automobiles, even though the United States maintains a 2.9 percent duty and the European Community has a 10.8 percent duty on imports.

2) In fiscal year 1981, import duties on automobile parts will be abolished as a general policy of the Japanese government.

3) Japan has no quantitative restrictions on auto imports.

4) The Japanese government has greatly simplified the inspection and certification systems for foreign imports. Inspectors will be sent overseas and the inspection time will be reduced.

5) Finally, the application of Japan's strict oxides of nitrogen emission standard established in 1978 was delayed for foreign-made cars three years behind the schedule for domestic autos.

Japan does maintain a commodity tax on automobiles based on engine size, but this is applied uniformly to domestic and imported autos alike. In concept, it is no different from the bias against large cars that has been built into American laws such as the Energy Tax Act of 1978 and the Energy Policy and Conservation Act of 1975.

While the Japanese distribution system does pose problems for foreign producers, this is the result of custom and the evolution of our business system, rather than a deliberate effort to exclude imports from our market. I am confident that American and other foreign auto makers can overcome these distribution problems, but to do so will require a sustained, long-term effort to sell vehicles that are adapted to the Japanese market.

Finally, far from making no contribution to the American economy, I believe the Japanese companies, and other importers, make a very sizable contribution indeed. A 1979 study by Harbridge House shows that the importing and retailing sectors of the U.S. imported automobile industry:

1) account for 138,000 jobs in this country;
2) are wholly responsible for the creation of some 5,000 independent businesses, and are partially responsible for an additional 1,850 independent businesses;
3) have stimulated nearly $3 billion in net investments and hundreds of millions of dollars annually in purchases of materials, components and services;
4) and pay well over half a billion dollars annually in tax revenues.

In summary, rather than the negative view many Americans hold about our role in the current problems facing the U.S. auto industry, we tend to view it as relatively neutral; that we are the temporary beneficiaries of events beyond our control much as the American industry has temporarily suffered from events beyond its control. We do not claim any special foresight, but neither do we accept the blame for the current problem.

Now for the second half of my topic—Reaching an Accommodation. In view of these widely different perspectives between our countries on the auto trade question, what type of "accommodation" can be reached in our trade relations?

I believe that the "accommodation"—to be satisfactory to all of us—must be fashioned to the long-term conditions of the world automobile market and not be an over-reaction to short-term problems. These long-term conditions that I refer to include competitive harmony in the small car market and the movement toward the concept of a "world car."

You will not be surprised to hear that I do not believe the impostition of U.S. auto import barriers meets the criteria for an "accommodation" that I just outlined. There are at least four reasons for this:

1) I do not believe that restrictions on U.S. auto imports will result in a net gain in domestic employment. A study that Nissan commissioned from Resource Assessment, Inc., in late 1979 shows that if 25 percent of Datsun sales were switched to domestic cars as a result of import quotas, approximately 9,600 direct and indirect jobs would be lost in the United States. And if 25 percent of all import sales were replaced by domestic vehicles, some 22,500 jobs would be lost. In fact, according to U.S. Department of Labor statistics, there is a very weak connection between auto imports and layoffs of auto workers in this country. The vast majority of unemployed workers had worked in plants producing large and intermediate size cars and trucks.

2) Auto import restrictions would have an extremely negative impact on consumers. The Council of Economic Advisors estimated last year that a reduction in Japanese auto imports of 500,000 units would cost the American consumers nearly $4 billion or about $90,000 for every unemployed auto worker who might regain a job in the domestic industry. Moreover, the estimated 5-7 percent increase in new car prices would further depress an already weak domestic market. Finally, the income generated by this reduction in imports would be highly skewed toward the major U.S. auto maker with only minimal benefit for the others.

3) U.S. import barriers would run contrary to American policies designed to cut inflation and reduce dependence on oil imports.

4) The imposition of auto import restrictions, especially in light of the recent U.S. International Trade Commission ruling, would be a clear signal to the rest of the world that the United States is turning protectionist. There is little need for me to comment on how this would affect Japan. But it should also be noted that protectionism here could have enormously adverse consequences for American auto makers and other U.S. industries. For example:

It could easily lead to an intensification of auto import restrictions worldwide, blocking American exports from foreign markets just as your industry is beginning to produce highly competitive vehicles;

it might lead to "upstream" trade barriers on auto parts at the same time that the U.S. auto makers are pioneering the concept of "world cars," including global sourcing of components;

and it could lead to foreign retaliation against the products of many of your export industries at the same time that your government has launched a major effort to help U.S. companies crack foreign markets.

In my view, import restrictions would be an extremely expensive way to provide the U.S. auto industry minor relief from a temporary problem.

If import restrictions are not the way to go, what is? I would say that an "accommodation"—that is, a mutual contribution to the resolution of the auto trade problem—is already being made.

For instance, on the American side, the U.S. auto makers are in the process of committing some $80 billion—an unprecedented sum—to modernization and retooling to meet the permanent market shift to small, fuel-efficient cars. As I noted earlier, this effort has already increased U.S. small car capacity by about two million units during the past two years. And the quality of these new cars is, in some cases, unsurpassed.

To the Japanese auto manufacturers, the scale of resources brought to producing a new generation of American cars is truly frightening. While we recognize that this investment has placed a heavy burden on the U.S. companies in the short run, we also fear that it could threaten our very existence in the longer term. What is more, the U.S. government appears to be fully behind your industry's effort in terms of reduced regulation, additional tax benefits, and more research and development assistance.

On the Japanese side, however, Japanese manufacturers are also making a new commitment to the American market. Nissan will soon break ground at its site in Tennessee for a $300 million investment in facilities to produce light trucks. Honda has already broken ground for its car assembly plant in Ohio. And Toyota, which now produces truck beds in California, is holding widely publicized discussions with Ford Motor Company on the question of joint production of vehicles in this country. Aside from the Japanese companies, of course, Volkswagen already operates a major facility in Pennsylvania, and Renault will be producing its vehicles in conjunction with American Motors in Wisconsin. In addition, Japanese auto makers are purchasing more American-made parts than ever before, and are continuing to investigate new opportunities to expand these domestic purchases.

Frankly speaking, we recognize that, under the current difficult circumstances, many Americans believe we have not done enough. But you will also understand that, as prudent businessmen, our decisions have to be based on economic reality and the long-term interests of our companies. We have several reservations about additional manufacturing plants in the United States, including:

First: the severe handicap we would face with relatively small production scales compared to the domestic manufacturers.

Second: the fact that any new facilities would come on stream just as the U.S. industry had finished its own retooling and would be turning out a high volume of small, fuel-efficient vehicles for its home market.

Third: our normal concerns about the costs of such an investment, and the quality and quantity of the supply of parts and components available to us in the United States.

In conclusion, I believe that the United States and Japan are already well on the way to reaching the type of "accommodation" in our auto trade relations that is appropriate to the problem now confronting the domestic industry. It is an "accommodation" that recognizes both the temporary nature of the difficult adjustment U.S. manufacturers are making to new market conditions and the long-term factors that will affect the development of the auto industry world-wide.

In closing, I would like to quote from the statement by Mr. Masataka Okuma, Executive Vice President, Nissan Motor Company, Ltd., given before the Automotive News World Congress this past summer, and I quote:

> In general, when an industry reaches a certain level of development, it becomes very difficult for the respective makers to exist and grow in an atmosphere of mutual prosperity. What usually happens at this stage is a shake-out, with fierce struggles breaking out for the desired share of a limited market.
>
> However, with regard to the automobile industry in particular, since it constitutes one of the basic industries in most industrialized countries, this purely survival-of-the-fittest approach may not be in the best interests of the economy of a country.
>
> Therefore, in the future we should strive to promote a system of "competitive harmony." That is, while continuing to maintain the free trade system based on the ideas of competition and cooperation, each country should try to promote its activities more harmoniously, that is, on a more mutual consensus.
>
> Please understand, the Japanese automobile industry, which at present accounts for nearly one-fourth of the world's automobile production, is fully conscious of its size and role in determining the future direction for the industry as a whole and would like to act in concert with the makers of other countries to achieve our mutual goals.

With that, ladies and gentlemen, I conclude. Thank you very much.

# LABOR AND THE JAPANESE CHALLENGE

## Donald F. Ephlin

I want to congratulate Secretary Goldschmidt and Undersecretary Beckham here for the fine report summarizing the problems facing the auto industry, including the Japanese challenge. I hope very sincerely that the new administration takes Secretary Goldschmidt's report as a starting point for their efforts to solve the problems facing this basic American industry.

In talking about the Japanese challenge, it is important to remember that Japanese auto manufacturers are not the supermen that the media seem to make them. They have done a fine job and deserve credit for it, but we ought to examine the total picture to understand what has happened.

When some American businessmen look at the Japanese situation, they only see certain parts of it—particularly the difference between Japanese and American autoworkers' wages. As Secretary Goldschmidt explained, the wage differential is at most one-third of the landed cost advantage that Japanese exporters have. A colleague of mine, just returned from Japan, talked with Japanese autoworkers there, and he feels that when we consider all the benefits paid to people over in Japan, including housing subsidies and all the rest, the true wage differential is minor.

If Americans, tending to oversimplify things and look for short-term answers, look only at the wage differential and decide that this is an opportune time to reduce the standard of living of American workers by one-third or one-half, I think we're in for some very, very difficult days ahead. But if we examine the total picture and sit down cooperatively to figure out solutions to our problems, I think that there are many things that can be done.

The American automobile industry is for the first time trying to compete directly with the Japanese. Up to a couple of years ago we never tried to compete with foreign imports, either European or Japanese. American auto companies were quite content to let imports have 10 to 15 percent of the small car market as long as they had the 85 percent which included all the big most profitable cars. Only recently have we started talking about world cars and direct competition.

Some of the things that have to be done will require a great deal of capital and are very complicated. But some of the most important advantages that the Japanese enjoy can be corrected for little or no cost. A National Science Foundation study that I'm involved in with some other people from the auto industry argues that the biggest advantage the Japanese have is their more efficient use of human resources. Many of our problems in that area can be corrected in cost effective ways if we do it properly. And of course the Japanese efforts to establish a national industrial policy and to plan for the long-term future can also be readily accomplished here by the administration's working with auto industry management; the UAW would certainly be happy to participate in those discussions.

The UAW's position on what legislation is needed is very close to what the Goldschmidt report outlines. We are presenting testimony today before congress advocating temporary restrictions on imports to allow time for the industry to turn around without a permanent loss of market.

In the longer term, however, we also think that there should be local content laws for high volume sellers. The U.S. domestic market is not only the biggest in the world, it's also the most open. More and more local content laws and restrictions are appearing world-wide; the Japanese themselves made arrangements in Italy to coproduce cars with Alfa Romeo that will have 75 percent Italian content. They are not allowed to flood the Italian market with Japanese automobiles, so they entered into that type of arrangement.

Other countries also have restrictions. Right now in Mexico many auto manufacturers are building plants because of Mexican local content laws; we will not sit by and see our jobs go to Mexico because they have such a law and we do not. If Ford, General Motors, Volkswagen, and others build all the engines that they propose to in Mexico, there will be enough engines produced there to satisfy a large part of the world auto market. We obviously cannot tolerate this type of situation.

Moreover, we think that every company has an obligation to provide jobs where it sells its products. Ford Motor Company and General Motors long ago went to Europe and built auto plants. We have not been exporting automobiles to Europe for many, many years. They went over there to build the cars that they sell there. Volkswagen, similarly, came to America. If a local content law is the only way to achieve equity in world trade situations, we think that is what is needed. The UAW has asked President-elect Reagan, incidentally, to convene a summit meeting on the auto industry problems as soon as he takes office. We must establish some national goals for this industry and other industries in difficult straits, such as steel.

At the company level there are many improvements that can be made, and we think the most promising involve increasing worker participation, in any number of ways. UAW President Douglas Fraser is now a member of the Board of Directors of Chrysler Corporation, and shortly we will have a member representing workers on the American Motors Company Board of Directors. (This should not be unfamiliar to the American companies, because in Europe it happens often; a former colleague of mine serves with distinction on the board of Ford of Germany.)

In the discussions going on today in Washington concerning the future of Chrysler Corporation, the UAW is talking not only about freezing wages but also about other corrective steps which must be taken to protect the people who work at Chrysler. In particular we are talking about a very expanded role for workers in the decision-making process; I would wager that any agreement reached between Chrysler and our union will include some provisions new to the auto industry which I think will be starting us in the right direction.

We must expand the role of the national auto industry committees like the quality of work life committee at General Motors that I've worked with since 1973. Our joint achievements at General Motors are revolutionary: what has been done was unthinkable only a few years ago. At Ford, management and the UAW now have a joint national committee on employee involvement; we are working together diligently to solve problems of quality and absenteeism. Incidentally, the quality of work life agreements that the UAW proposed and that management accepted back in 1973 included improving product quality as one of their main ingredients.

Troubled times bring people together, and I think we can cooperate in ways that were unthinkable a few years ago, but we're only scratching the surface; much more can be done, most importantly in labor-management relations on the plant floor. No one in America knows more about building automobiles than the UAW members who have been building quality cars for many years. But quality in the present set-up is determined largely by management. Workers do not make decisions on the quality of the products they build; those decisions are made by others.

American workers want to build quality products. I am now working with the Ford Motor Company to borrow back from the Japanese (I say it that way because it was not their idea originally) the production quality techniques that are serving them so well. Quality control circles are being established in almost every major Ford installation in North America. The working together part of the Japanese system is something we are learning to do successfully.

Let me turn to the point that's always mentioned last: that is the question of productivity. American auto workers can help improve productivity in their plants in many ways if they are given the opportunity. Those who examine the Japanese system quite often neglect to talk about it, but the Japanese have a primary goal of full employment in their country—something which the United States has not achieved in my lifetime except during war—and secondly they provide security for their workers. The UAW has always been willing to accept new machines and new technology to improve productivity; we've had robots in our plants for years before most of you heard about them. But to ask people to help improve productivity by eliminating their own jobs is really kind of unthinkable. We must provide new measures of security for workers if we want them to participate in improving productivity and making American industry more competitive.

National productivity, with the unemployment levels that we have tolerated in the United States for many years, obviously cannot be maximal. If we are to meet foreign competition in the auto industry in the long term we must improve productivity and must work cooperatively in solving those problems that confront us.

I believe we are at a crossroads as far as American labor-management relationships are concerned: we can either take advantage of the opportunities presented to us and sit down and work together, or we can continue to engage in senseless philosophical warfare and watch the industry that is the backbone of our economy wither away and die.

I hope we are equal to the challenge. I know that the people I'm privileged to represent are the best auto workers in the world, given the right opportunity, the right tools, and the right setting. They will do the job. Workers and their unions can contribute to restoring the health of the American auto industry. I think we ought to focus on our opportunities to improve this difficult situation and not cry about what is wrong or try to blame one another.

Thank you very much.

# THE AMERICAN AUTOMOBILE INDUSTRY
## AND THE JAPANESE CHALLENGE


### David S. Potter


When Dave Cole invited me to take part in this forum, he described it as "a quiet little gathering in Ann Arbor." Dave obviously has a gift for understatement. Nevertheless, I'm delighted to be here with you this morning and to serve in the same session with such distinguished colleagues.

My role in the forum is to give you the business perspective of the Japanese challenge and the impact that challenge has had on the American auto industry.

The title of the forum itself asks the question, "Is the Japanese auto industry a model and challenge for the future?" I think that the answer is pretty clear: the Japanese have good ideas in the way they produce their products. Some of their processes are specific to their culture and just don't transplant very well to American soil. Others are highly adaptable—and, where they promise improvement for our industry, many of them are _being_ adapted by American automakers.

So the Japanese very definitely _are_ providing U.S. auto manufacturers with a challenge. Their impact has been significant—second perhaps only to the oil shocks which have rocked our industry in recent years.

The numbers alone document the Japanese impact, and already this morning we've had a lot of them. However, I think two facts having to do with numbers are especially significant: first, the fact that in 1980, for the first time, Japan was the number one auto-producing nation; and, second, they currently are selling about 20 percent of the new cars in North America.

In the face of facts such as these, it's obvious that to meet the Japanese challenge, U.S. automakers must find ways to regain their customers and acquire new ones. Moreover, in doing so, we must also reduce costs to become more productive and more able competitors over the long term. There is no single solution, no single step that can be taken that will wipe out our cost disadvantage; a number of steps have to be taken, and taken essentially simultaneously. The ultimate goal is increased productivity to help us regain our competitive edge.

We can become more productive in a number of ways, and business, labor, and government in this country all have important roles to play. Business and labor must work together to reduce labor costs sensibly and fairly, to improve labor-management relations, and to bring our employees into a more informed and participative relationship. Management must review its own industrial practices and processes, some of which are less effficient than those employed by the Japanese. And government must review its industrial policies and find ways to encourage rather than discourage industrial development.

Now, I should caution you, when I say government has a role to play, I don't mean that role should be blatant protectionism. However, we believe that practices currently being followed by some Japanese vehicle producers are short-sighted and are generating pressures here in the United States, as well as in many other countries, that could result in lasting harm to important world trade relationships. We have urged our government to take the initiative in persuading the Japanese government to protect its own self-interest by acting immediately and voluntarily to adopt more prudent trade practices. Such prudence would appear critically urgent in light of the current groundswell of sentiment for rigid legislative solutions and restrictions which now seems to be building in this country.

Still, there's no doubt about it: meeting the productivity

challenge—the <u>real</u> challenge of the Japanese—will be a tremendous, even formidable task. The size of the problem is so great that almost any magazine or newspaper you pick up these days is full of gloom and doom about our industry.

Don't be taken in by the negativism. Sure, a lot of changes have to be made by U.S. automakers, but remember ours is an industry that lives by change—literally thrives on it. Speaking for General Motors, I can assure you, we at GM are committed to making the changes that are necessary. We have already begun—and with a giant-size effort.

Yet it's important to remember, the goal is a stronger, more competitive U.S. auto industry—not a clone of the Japanese model. That would be impossible, even if we wanted it, and we don't. As others have noted, we can hardly import Japanese culture wholesale into this country—but we can pick out the best features the Japanese industry has to offer, combine these with the unique and outstanding features of our industry, and produce a revitalized American car and truck industry—greater than any of the ingredients that went into it.

As I say, this process is going on right now. We are examining all the things we know about automaking in Japan, and we are seeking out ways to Americanize their best systems—to apply in our industry the practices and processes that have been so productive for the Japanese, just as they have taken and adapted our practices and technology. Let me give you a few examples.

We are dramatically increasing the use of robots in our factories. By 1985, we expect some 5,000 robots will be in use at GM, and by 1990, the number will grow to about 14,000. We are studying new ferrous metal casting technology and making a full conversion to computer-controlled paint booths. We are additionally employing the new Computer Command Control electronic technology now found in all GM gasoline-powered cars to complete final inspections in the assembly plant.

We are re-examining virtually all of the "givens" in making a car. The rapid-die-change technology being used by the Japanese is undergoing a close look at General Motors. If we can successfully introduce this process in our plants, we will get greater production from existing presses and thereby reduce future investment requirements. The Japanese practice of assembling cars in smaller plants is also being reviewed. Smaller plants to do the same work are potentially much more efficient and therefore more desirable. However, at the same time, we believe it's important to provide our employees a pleasing environment in which to work—an environment that includes the wider aisles, better lighting, and other modern features commonly found in newer American auto plants.

We are also scrutinizing the carefully orchestrated Japanese inventory-management system, the just-in-time system known as Kan-Ban, to see if at least some of its features are applicable at General Motors. This system typically relies on a network of suppliers within close proximity of the manufacturing facility. It also operates on a high degree of trust between supplier and manufacturer rather than the endless counting of inventory we're accustomed to.

One of the beneficial side effects of all this modernization is that we're gaining far better control over the quality of products made in our plants. Higher quality—and better quality control—are the natural result of greater automation and mechanization. A machine that's programmed to perform a tedious job over and over again <u>automatically</u> just doesn't get as tired as a human auto worker—and, therefore, it doesn't make as many mistakes.

That's one of the main reasons for installing robots—not so much for their labor-saving properties as for their ability to improve quality control. Furthermore, with robots making fewer mistakes, fewer inspectors may be needed, and that's another boon. Putting a lot of inspectors in the plant really doesn't contribute all that much to product quality anyway. You can't <u>inspect</u> quality in; you've got to <u>build</u> it in—and robots are helping us to do that.

Lest it be forgotten, I want to point out that quality itself contributes to increased productivity. It's no coincidence that the

Japanese auto industry is both very productive—and very quality-conscious. By the same token, I think U.S. manufacturers in many industries are paying a lot more attention these days to improving quality and customer satisfaction. We certainly are at General Motors. We're designing our products from the ground up with quality foremost in our minds, and in recent years we've appointed both a vice president for consumer relations and service and a vice president for quality and reliability. More than ever, quality has become a top-level priority at General Motors. Virtually all the elements of the quality equation are being re-evaluated, beginning with our suppliers and the factory and extending right down to the auto dealership.

Management in the auto industry is not alone in attempting to meet the Japanese challenge of higher productivity. To its credit, organized labor is also getting more and more involved in the effort. In the past year or so, we've seen our major unions working much harder at achieving more harmonious relationships with management—much as is the norm in Japan. In a world where we're fighting for industrial survival and where both labor and business are going to sink or ride out the storm in the same boat, it is essential that we work together to make sure that we get through.

As a consequence, labor and management today are more inclined to work constructively together to reduce labor costs. We're trying to do this by introducing more robotics and more automation in an orderly fashion and by doing a better job of managing our business. We must get away from any of the efficiency-limiting agreements of the past and instead start talking more about reducing costs and about the greater good.

A vital key to better labor management, of course, is the effort to involve the workers themselves more in the industrial process. We start with the premise that the American worker is as good as any worker in the world. And it's increasingly clear that American workers today want more involvement with their jobs; they want to know more about management's problems and they want to take on greater responsibility. When they do—the result usually is that they do better at their jobs. They get more things right the first time around, and they're just as happy about the savings this represents as we are.

The Japanese have understood the need for worker involvement for many years, and their efforts in that direction through use of the Quality Circles have been well documented.

In similar fashion, American industry has also been striving for greater worker participation. These efforts have intensified, and General Motors has been the industry leader in the U.S. in this movement.

We are approaching the goal of greater worker involvement at General Motors primarily through broad-based efforts to improve the quality of work life for our employees. Virtually every GM location now has some kind of quality-of-work-life effort under way. About 80 GM locations have gone a step further and have established joint union-management operations dedicated to QWL improvements. I might add that early results from these efforts have been just outstanding.

Finally, there is that role for government that I spoke about earlier. Here, too, I think we can see that progress is being made. One of the not-so-secret weapons the Japanese have had for many years is the unusually cooperative relationship they have with their government. Official government policy in Japan is to support and encourage business—but such a supportive government policy has been sadly lacking in the United States for years.

With a new national administration coming into power next week in Washington, we are hopeful that this will be changed—that a more peaceful, harmonious relationship will be fostered between government and business in this country. There is a great deal that our government can do—and should do—if it wants to encourage the growth of business and in so doing, to help assure the economic viability of the nation.

Let me enumerate some of the improvements we believe are necessary.

In general, government policymakers should provide a better climate for investment in American business by encouraging greater capital formation for new plants and equipment and for research and development. They can do this by revising the tax laws to allow a faster write-off of capital equipment and by lowering corporate as well as individual tax rates to encourage more investment. Government policy makers should also work to eliminate excessive and counter-productive regulations which inhibit our ability to compete successfully in world markets. Reducing inflation, striking a better balance between our monetary and fiscal policies, and cutting back spending will also contribute greatly to the resurgence of business. It is not enough for the auto manufacturers alone to get well; the entire basic industrial complex must get well. This, of course, would include all the suppliers to the auto industry, whose costs must also be competitive on a worldwide basis.

For years we in American business have been hearing that one of the reasons the Japanese succeed is that they're more willing to take the long view—to stress long-term financial returns over the short-term. The inverse proposition is that U.S. industry has been hurt by its predisposition to short-term financial results. However, I have to say that it's been extremely difficult for American business to take a long-term view of its investment when some government agencies—particularly the IRS—take such an extremely short-range view of life, forcing us to do the same. A more responsive, supportive attitude on the part of our government could easily change this—and we're hoping that will happen during the course of the next four years.

Summing it all up, we believe that the U.S. auto industry is reacting to the crisis of high-priced fuel and the Japanese challenge. With the help of government and of labor, we are stepping up to the competitive challenge of the Japanese and other foreign competitors. We are becoming more productive, more quality-conscious, more responsive to the needs of our customers and our own employees. We are becoming a leaner and stronger industry, and we look forward to competing on a world-wide basis with the Japanese—and any other comers—for years to come.

# THE AMERICAN AUTOMOBILE INDUSTRY
# AND THE JAPANESE CHALLENGE

Fred G. Secrest

From the perspective of the American automotive industry, there's certainly no question that the Japanese represent a very real and immediate challenge. And this view is not limited to the United States. Pick up a newspaper in London, Paris, Bonn, Rome, or even Stockholm and it will be clear that European auto producers also consider the challenge from Japan to be fundamental.

There's an important difference, however, between the European and American views of this challenge. Many Americans see the Japanese challenge as only a short-term phenomenon. Wait a few months, they say—until the 1981 U.S. models become established, or until the 1982 models are introduced—and the tide of imports will recede about as fast as it rose. Most Europeans, on the other hand, seem convinced that the race has just begun—and they're dead right.

This morning, I'd like to focus on the Japanese challenge and the types of U.S. responses it requires. Some of these can draw upon business and governmental policies proven to be effective in Japan. I'm thinking of both the managerial aspects—such as product quality, labor relations, and productivity—and the highly-effective relationship between Japanese business and government.

This afternoon's agenda deals at length with quality, productivity, and technology. Japan has developed a variety of brilliant techniques in each of these areas; we know, because we have been studying them very hard lately. I'd like to make four brief points on these subjects:

First, we can adopt many of these Japanese techniques; after all, many of the basic ideas were borrowed from the United States in the first place. Of course this doesn't mean that the job will be quick or easy; unique geography, supplier relationships, and cultural traditions play important roles in the Japanese automotive system.

Second, U.S. producers and the UAW are committed and working hard to improve quality and productivity; the enormous investments being made in new facilities will provide major contributions in both areas.

Third, 9 out of 10 of today's owners say they are satisfied with their U.S. cars, so much of the public perception of U.S. quality may be an image problem; we could use a lot more of the favorable press we've started to see on the new U.S. models.

Fourth, U.S. techonology—be it front-drive cars, transaxles, electronics, or robotic techniques—takes a back seat to nobody. Nevertheless, this is a fast track open to all producers, and we can't rely on technology alone to overcome fundamental business problems.

If quality and technology were the only arenas where U.S. and Japanese cars will contest, the outlook for U.S. auto production would be bright, indeed. But, the list is much broader. In the short-term, the dominant issue is the momentum of Japanese imports. Longer term, the overriding issue is competitive costs.

Let's look at the short-term outlook first. It's no secret that 1980 was a very bad year for the U.S. auto industry. Retail sales of domestic cars and trucks were at a 19-year low of 8.3 million units. For the first nine months, General Motors, Ford, and Chrysler each lost $1.5 billion before taxes. In two years' time, almost 2,300 domestic dealers have gone out of business and some 140 parts plants have been closed. And, for most of last year, the effects of auto unemployment have been costing the American economy close to one million jobs.

Such widespread misery was, of course, not caused by imports alone. Recession, high-priced gasoline, soaring interest rates and inflation, the near-collapse of the truck market, and the mix shift to smaller cars all took their toll. But multiple wounds certainly don't make the injury from surging imports any easier to bear.

I'm sure everyone here knows the statistics on imports. In terms of car market share, they've almost doubled in the past four years—from 14.8 percent in 1976 to 26.5 percent in 1980. Japanese cars have soared from a 9.3 percent share in 1976 to 21.1 percent in 1980. For Japan, this increase was worth one million extra car sales last year, even in a year of major recession. For U.S. taxpayers, the cost was almost $3 billion in extra unemployment benefits and lost tax revenues. And it cost U.S. auto producers $1.5 billion in lost profits and 200,000 lost jobs in the industry (including suppliers). It's not surprising, then, that Congress is concerned and that there is considerable grass-roots support for some form of import restriction.

There isn't much question about why this surge in Japanese share occurred. Suddenly, with the Iranian revolution in the spring of 1979, U.S. car buyers became convinced that expensive gasoline was a reality—and the small-car share of our market rose very sharply. Japan—having lived with high gasoline prices for years—had always concentrated on small cars and had been steadily raising production capacity for auto exports. So Japan was ready for the shift in U.S. auto demand—without the huge costs and delays involved in retooling its products and plants.

Why U.S. producers had not been able to forecast the fall of the Shah and become more prepared can be debated forever, but there's blame enough for all sectors to share. The issue now is what to do about it. The American firms know what types of products are needed and how to design and build them. They are well into an $80 billion program to convert the entire U.S. car fleet to get fuel economy averaging 30 mpg or better by 1985. But this takes time and capital—capital that should be flowing in <u>now</u> from sales of U.S. cars and trucks which, instead, are being lost to imports and recession.

Although the near-term outlook is bleak, history suggests that factors such as recession and abnormally high interest rates only <u>postpone</u> auto demand that will be made up when the economy improves. Unfortunately, the same prospect for recovery does not apply when U.S. car sales are lost to imports. Satisfied owners are repeat buyers; which causes sales lost to imports today to repeat as sales losses in the future—especially after dealer failures have shrunk the retail sales capacity of U.S. producers.

What's needed is for U.S. producers to reverse the sales momentum of imports and to regain their own momentum. But let's face the facts, this reversal has <u>not</u> occurred. For the last 60 days, the annual rate of import sales has averaged more than 2.5 million cars, slightly higher than for 1980 as a whole.

In spite of the strength of import sales, I'm delighted to report that Ford's new Escort and Lynx models are selling very well; we're running at capacity on these products, and they're outselling the strongest of the import models. But two or three new model successes can't carry the whole U.S. industry; we have to sell the full line of U.S. small cars.

The average fuel economy of this U.S. fleet of small cars is now within 2 or 3 miles-per-gallon of the Japanese competitors; and U.S. producers have capacity to build almost 5 1/2 million of these models this year. But, even with most of the right products available for today's market, it's going to take time to get customers back into domestic showrooms. This is the immediate challenge.

I mentioned Europe earlier because the experience with Japanese imports there suggests what we face in this country. Like the Japanese, the Europeans have specialized in smaller cars, and heavy taxes have kept gasoline prices high. Thus, Europe did not encounter the sudden <u>shift</u> in demand that provided Japan such a windfall in the United States. Moreover, the external auto tariff in the Common Market is about five times (or $450 a unit above) the U.S. rate; and several major European nations have placed limits on Japanese car imports—11 percent of the market in Britain; 3 percent in France; just token entries allowed in Italy and Spain.

Outside of these countries, the Japanese are now getting 11 percent of the West German market and 24 percent of the rest of Western Europe. So—without the help of a sudden market switch, and in spite of relatively high tariffs—the Japanese are achieving shares in the non-restricted parts of Europe that, on average, are about as high as their U.S. share. This certainly suggests caution in making predictions about rolling back Japan's share in the United States as new American cars come into production.

Of course, to succeed at all, these new U.S. cars will have to be fully competitive with the Japanese in quality and technology, and I'm confident that U.S. producers can meet these goals. But the cost of producing cars in the United States also must be competitive with Japanese cars; otherwise car production in this country inevitably will wane.

U.S. production costs are not competitive today. It seems probable that a Japanese car can be landed in the United States today for at least $1,000, or 25 percent, below the U.S. cost of producing a similar car. Many factors contribute to this American disadvantage, but the major ones are compensation and productivity. The U.S. auto industry doesn't need editorials to tell us that this problem has to be tackled, and I fully expect to see important progress made—but such progress will not come easily or quickly. Moreover, we're shooting at a moving target; high U.S. inflation and (until very recently) a relatively weak yen have caused the U.S. cost disadvantage to double since 1978.

A major realignment of the yen/dollar relationship certainly would help. The Europeans claim the yen is undervalued by 20-25 percent because of Japan's oil vulnerability and its controls over international transactions. Perhaps, too, the dollar's role as a reserve currency artificially inflates the exchange value of our own currency. Whether or not these points are valid, a major and permanent change in yen/dollar values would have very large economic and political consequences in both America and Japan. Consequently, we probably shouldn't count on too much help from this factor to regain our competitive position.

Nor can the vitally needed changes in U.S. tax and regulatory policy be relied on to eliminate our cost disadvantage. Certainly the United States needs to cut inflation, reduce taxes, spur investment, and make regulations more cost-effective. But such improvements will do more to avoid future penalties (and to conserve vital capital) than to eliminate today's cost disadvantage.

Volkswagen's and Renault's decisions to produce in the United States indicate that car production costs in Europe are similar to those in America—and thus, Europe faces much the same competitive cost disadvantage relative to Japan as we do. The European Community is looking at placing further quantitative limits on Japanese imports to supplement its high auto tariff, because most European governments long ago decided that a healthy auto sector is fundamental to their national economies. It seems that Americans would also like a healthy national auto industry, but few of our leaders appear ready to endorse the policy changes required to get there. I think the Japanese know this, which may be why the United States is such a magnet for Japanese auto exports.

Why do the Japanese seem to grapple so effectively with these problems while we continue to flounder and argue? Without advocating that America copy Japan's model for business-government relationship, we might learn something by examining three aspects of the Japanese approach.

First, style. By and large, private and public relationship in Japan are oriented toward consensus, while the U.S. relationship far too often is adversarial. The Japanese style leads to working out problems in a pragmatic fashion instead of encouraging legalistic confrontations and wasteful trials of strength in the political, judicial, and media arenas. I'm encouraged that both business and government now seem to recognize this and have placed a more constructive relationship high on the national agenda.

Second, <u>goal setting</u>. Promoting sound economic growth is accepted as a goal in Japan, and I hope the recent elections have helped (if help was needed) to reaffirm such a goal for the United States. But the Japanese then go on to outline the means of accomplishing such growth in specific sectors of the economy. For too long, America has taken its industrial strength for granted. Now, we seem to agree that urgent attention is needed to re-establish a world-class industrial base. But we need to go beyond a <u>general</u> awakening and confront the <u>specific actions</u> by industry, government, and labor to restore U.S. industrial vigor. In motor vehicles, industry and labor know what they have to do; the open issue is the role of government.

And third, the Japanese are <u>consistent</u>—they are more successful than the Americans in integrating the various elements of policy needed to reach their goals. In the early 1950s, Japan set a world-scale auto industry as a major national goal. Thereafter, the motor vehicle industry became eligible for a variety of special financing, tax, and export incentives—in addition to benefitting from general policies such as taxation favoring capital generation and prolonged defense of a cheap yen. These policies created the opportunity for auto industry development that was then assured by Japan's auto trade policy. For 20 years, foreign competition was rigorously excluded through import quotas, extraordinary tariffs and special taxes, and a ban on foreign automotive investment in Japan.

The obvious question is whether we should adopt some of these Japanese policies. Last year's events certainly have made U.S. auto policy a public issue, and some have responded that the United States should get out of the auto business if we can't compete on our own. Others, while they agree with this advice "in principle," also recognize its catastrophic employment implications. But still they stand apart from any concrete action, apparently in the hope somehow that something will stem the tide of imports until U.S. auto producers can adjust to the Japanese challenge. Unfortunately, we're fresh out of <u>somehows</u> and <u>somethings</u>. Moreover, adjustment certainly will not be successful if the hemorrhaging of U.S. car volume, cash flow, and jobs continues.

The time has come to choose: either to stand aside complete-ly, or to face the auto import threat squarely with new policies that will enable the U.S. industry to adjust to Japanese competition. Either choice requires government action, because U.S. auto policy today is <u>not</u> "hands-off." Advocates of abandoning a domestic auto industry to its own devices surely should also insist that all con-straints be removed: repeal the local content rules imposed on domestic producers under the fuel-economy law; refuse special aid to any of the participants; eliminate U.S. tariffs on cars, parts and materials, including steel.

But before this choice is made, let's make certain that other sectors <u>in fact,</u> and not just in theory, will take up the employment slack, and that the United States can truly afford to import most of its automotive requirements. Let's also understand why Japan and Europe have decided that they <u>need</u> strong auto industries, while the United States—which carries much of the economic burden of de-fending them <u>and</u> us—seems unsure about it. If the social, trade, and national welfare costs of complete laissez-faire turn out to be unac-ceptable—and Congress seems to think they are—then let's stop all the theoretical arguments and get on with policies to restore economic health to the auto industry.

These should include relief, not only on taxation and regula-tions, but also on trade. Most Americans agree that Japan <u>should</u> moderate its auto exports until the U.S. industry gets back on its feet. Further, the Japanese government supports this approach and seems to be waiting for the U.S. government to ask; I hope that the new Administration will do so promptly. Voluntary restraint may well offer the best opportunity for immediate gains in U.S. jobs and production, with no penalty to taxpayers in America and no risk of retaliation overseas.

Temporary restraint would provide time to convert more of the U.S. car fleet, and to make important progress on quality, pro-ductivity, and technology, but it should not be a permanent policy. For the longer term, Japanese auto producers ought to balance their U.S. sales with large-scale investment in U.S. plants and jobs. This has been the long-standing international policy of U.S. auto producers and, more recently, of the European producers as well. Even the Japanese government has offered some mild advocacy of such a program.

There must be a better way to accomplish this than to exclude imports for a generation, as did Japan; or to levy high tariffs, as in Europe (and Canada); or to enact local content laws, as in most other major auto markets. These unilateral approaches do work, of course; but so does our bilateral Auto Pact with Canada. It has endured remarkably well for 15 years, even though each side has been unhappy periodically—that, in itself, suggests it's been a reasonable deal for all parties.

The essence of the Auto Pact is to obtain reasonable balance in auto trade by setting the ground-rules, applicable to everyone alike, for market participation. It sets the conditions of competition without regulating how individual firms may elect to operate—and it's essentially a voluntary arrangement. The success of the Auto Pact can be measured by more efficient production in both countries, wider customer choice of models at relatively lower prices in Canada, and bilateral auto trade that has soared from $1 billion in 1965 to $22 billion last year.

Innovative concepts such as the Auto Pact require initiatives by governments, if only because of our stringent antitrust laws, but this does not mean that the ideas themselves must come from government. "Challenge" seems to be the word-of-the-day, and I'd like to issue one of my own. Let us put some first-class brains and major effort into developing a serious, carefully-crafted, and flexible U.S.-Japan automotive arrangement that will be of long-run benefit to both countries.

The time for polemics is past. The problem won't solve itself. This seems recognized by impartial observers in both countries. Mr. Amaya, Vice-Minister of MITI, has said, "In my opinion, voluntary restraints by Japanese automakers have been possible since about the beginning of 1980—if the present state of affairs continues, the conclusion of an orderly marketing agreement or the implementation of safeguards may be desirable. . . . the most important requirement for maintaining the free-trade system is to avoid driving one's competitors into a corner; otherwise . . . the system will self-destruct." That's a responsible, if personal and thus unofficial, Japanese viewpoint. From the American side, Professor Ezra Vogel—certainly no protectionist or captive-of-Detroit—has offered some refreshingly specific suggestions for new automotive arrangements. Why don't we move to a creative dialogue and a constructive solution to this most serious economic and political division between two of the strongest nations of the Free World?

# RESPONSES OF CONFERENCE PANELISTS
## TO AUDIENCE QUESTIONS

Panelists for the morning question and answer session were William BECKHAM, Jr., Deputy Secretary, U.S. Department of Transportation; Donald EPHLIN, Vice-President, United Automobile Workers; Paul W. McCRACKEN, Edmund Ezra Day Distinguished University Professor of Business Administration, The University of Michigan; David S. POTTER, Vice-President and Group Executive of the Public Affairs Group, General Motors Corporation; Fred G. SECREST, Consultant and Former Executive Vice-President, Environmental Safety and Industry Affairs, Ford Motor Company; and Yasuhiko SUZUKI, Vice-President, Nissan Motor Corporation, USA.

Q: What is the Reagan administration expected to do with the Goldschmidt report?

BECKHAM: The new administration has expressed a strong interest in dealing with the auto industry's problems. Transportation Secretary-designate Drew Lewis, in his confirmation hearing, stated that he thought the industry's difficulties would be the department's number-one concern. Therefore one would think that if our report is as good as some have indicated, the incoming administration might well take it as a starting point. I believe the report is very good. Its recommendations are far-reaching: if they were followed up on completely it would be of great benefit to the industry and its workers. The recommendations touch on probably every significant

51

aspect of the auto industry's situation, and we left open questions of which specific programs to implement. The new administration can use this report as a cornerstone and still have plenty of room to develop its own programs.

Q: Does General Motors endorse the Goldschmidt report's recommendations?

POTTER: Overall, General Motors believes the Department of Transportation study to be a thorough review of the industry's current situation. Moreover, we agree with the basic thrust of the report and many of its recommendations. We disagree, however, with the study's overly conservative assessment of worldwide industry growth potential.

General Motors has stated on numerous occasions that our government should encourage Japan voluntarily to adopt more prudent trade practices during this critical time of transition for U.S. domestic auto manufacturers. We therefore believe careful consideration should be given to the Department of Transportation's recommendation that our government undertake discussions with the Japanese government. Such voluntary action by the Japanese would help to abate growing protectionist pressures which threaten the fragile structure of international trade.

Q: What are the negative consequences for the United States of restricting Japanese auto imports? What is the least harmful method that might be employed?

McCRACKEN: The major negative consequences are those which always occur when trade is restricted. This narrows and weakens the scope for competition. In the longer run this must mean a weakening of the forces making for economic progress. Just because this case comes close to home for us in Michigan does not invalidate the general proposition. The stronger case that can be made for restraints on auto imports is that they should exist temporarily to give the domestic industry some time to re-tool for the new market. A case can be made that they are heavily the victims of a mismanaged energy policy and government now owes them a little insulation from foreign competition for which they would have been better prepared had market forces all along been in operation. While theoretically a tariff has a less disturbing effect on the economy than other forms of import restraints, in this case I should think the more informal the arrangement, the better, in order that it hopefully can be kept on a temporary basis. Once a trade restraint is legislated, it is difficult to remove.

Q: The U.S. - Canada automobile pact was suggested as an illustration of how two nations could work out a bilateral trade agreement; are there some things in that agreement which might give us some ideas for stabilizing the international automobile market?

SECREST: I think it would be misleading to state that the conditions that made a pact possible between the United States and Canada (a bilateral pact on a single product line as an adjunct to the overall GATT system) are sufficiently like those found in the U.S. - Japan automobile trade situation to guarantee that those same approaches could be successfully applied to bilateral auto trade between Japan and the United States.

On the face of it the U.S. - Canada situation was more promising to begin with: The companies were substantially the same, the union was largely the same and the language was mostly (not entirely!) the same. The geography was easier, and the product lines were closer together. Nevertheless, when that effort started it was considered doomed by most knowledgeable people on both sides. To make it work, certain things had to be recognized at the beginning. One is that it had to be entered into voluntarily by the two nations and could not be imposed by either nation against the other. It would have to be a set of rules that was accepted by both governments as in the long-run best interest of at least the majority of the producers and workers in both countries, or it would not work.

Because those interests differ, agreement won't come easily. After a while, however, people may begin to think that rather than battling to extinction there ought to be a better way.

A pact would involve flexibility rather than absolute numbers. It would, I think, involve a degree of voluntarism, so that people could operate outside the pact if they chose not to take advantage of whatever benefits it would add.

Essentially, it would provide, I think, for some commitment on the part of Japanese automotive manufacturers to add some portion of value in the United States if they wanted to sell in this market above some non-zero level. I would think that they might add this portion by any means they choose. This is the case in Canada. You do not have to produce there some portion of all the models of cars and trucks you may wish to sell; you may choose to produce some entire models there: Ford does, and I think General Motors also, produce a hundred percent of certain models in Canada. That kind of scale-economy operation will generate a reasonable amount of employment and promote trade balance.

Q: Would you describe some of Nissan's plans for the truck plant in Smyrna, Tennessee, with respect to such considerations as size of the labor force, component's domestic content, etc.?

SUZUKI: The Smyrna, Tennessee, truck assembly plant when in full operation will employ approximately 2,200 production workers. The initial level of U.S. manufacturer and component content is to be 40 percent.

Q: Could you be more specific on what role the workers should play in participating in what heretofore have been traditional management prerogatives (for example, decisions to locate new plants in Mexico)?

EPHLIN: We feel workers should participate in all decisions which have impact on their jobs. On the matter of sub-contracting and out-sourcing to foreign subsidiaries, there is no question but that workers may be able to point out sound reasons for keeping the jobs in-house. If workers are to be asked to share in the sacrifices needed to keep a company viable, they should not be providing capital to eliminate their own jobs.

Q: What do you recommend as ways to provide economic security to workers displaced by technological developments such as will occur with the coming introduction of robotics?

EPHLIN: Obviously the best way to provide economic security to workers is to have an expanding national economy which will continue to provide more and more jobs to people. Failure to improve our economy will leave us with no alternative but to further reduce working time to share available jobs.

Q: General Motors is said not to favor protectionism, but does think that there are some short-run, short-sighted Japanese government policies that need to be changed. What are some of these changes?

POTTER: The specific issue concerning trade protectionism that we at General Motors have been addressing our attention to for a year now is the long-term effect of some emergency legislative "fix" or formal written trade agreement. These things have a way of staying in position and not being backed off.

I think that in that case, the long-term effect on the United States and on all U.S. industries could be very bad. We should be striving for a freer trading economy in the world (at least in the free world we should be going in that direction), and anything that would promote long-term protectionism is not in the best interest of the United States.

However, in the short-term the domestic auto industry is experiencing genuine cash-flow problems. There's no point in trying to investigate funding an $80 billion capital investment program from today's money market, so it will have to be done largely out of cash flow. General Motors does advocate U.S. - Japanese government cooperation to seek some sort of voluntary restraints on exports, but we have avoided recommending any specific areas for negotiation, so as not to add to the present confusion about what constitutes a solution to this problem. We have newly elected officials and appointed officials who are supposed to lead such negotiations on the behalf of the United States, and I think that's a task that they should begin.

Q: The Japanese auto industry has accepted quantitative limits on its exports to the United Kingdom, France, and Italy. Why should it be unwilling to accept similar limits, temporarily, on exports to the United States?

SUZUKI: Well, regarding the restraint agreements with those European countries, I have never heard of any written code to restrain Japanese exports to those countries. However, personally, I am against any kind of restraint because I doubt that import restraints will help your economy in this country. I have some interesting figures with me: in 1979 the American domestic passenger automobile sales figure was 8,328,055 units; the same figure for 1980 was 6,578,252 units. That means American passenger car sales went down about 1.75 million units. To compare with these figures, import sales increased about 66,000 units between 1979 and 1980, which means that imports took only 3.8 percent of the total, reduced, American passenger car sales. Also I remember Undersecretary Beckham in a speech in Toledo, Ohio, last year, made a statement to the effect that the inroads from the Japanese into the American automobile market, although painful, may be of a short duration.

Actually, two major developments were responsible for the current market deterioration in this country. Number one is a shift in consumer demand from large cars to small cars, due to the energy crisis, and the American automobile manufacturers were unable to meet the demand for small, fuel-efficient cars because of insufficient supply.

Second, there was a decline in total demand for automobiles due to the slowdown in the American economy which began in 1979. As I stated in my speech, in the past two years the American manufacturers came up with a two-million unit increase in their capacity to produce small cars; however, very unluckily, when Detroit started responding to the consumer demand, they were faced with very high interest rates and a general economic downturn. These things have had the greatest single, serious effect on American domestic automobile sales.

So once these things are solved, I believe the American automobile sales will get healthier.

EPHLIN: Could I just point out one thing? It has been announced that production of the most fuel efficient automobile made in America by General Motors, the Chevette, is going to be reduced, and Chrysler's Omni and Horizon plant in Belvidere, Illinois, is closed at the moment for lack of sales. So we have unused capacity for the smallest, most fuel efficient automobiles in the country.

Q: Mr. Suzuki alleges no relation between imports and unemployment in the United States. Mr. Secrest attributes 200,000 unemployed to imports. Could you comment on this contradiction?

McCRACKEN: It is difficult to believe that the surge of imported automobiles has made no contribution to unemployment in the United States. At the same time, it would not be fair to assume that all of the unemployment is caused by these imported vehicles. There undoubtedly would be some people who, if the smaller imported vehicles had not been available, would have bought American cars. At the same time, it would be wrong to assume that if all imports had been prohibited, that additional number of domestic vehicles would have been purchased in their place.

Q: With inventories for Chevettes and Citations sometimes reaching or exceeding 100 days' supply and the K-car production schedules below expectations for the winter of 1980-81, how can you claim that the Japanese are merely temporarily filling the gap between domestic supply and demand for small fuel efficient cars?

SUZUKI: The point that I was making was that Japanese cars entered the U.S. market together with other imported cars by selling cars that domestic manufacturers preferred not to sell. For many years, imports competed for a small share of the U.S. market, namely the market for small, fuel-efficient cars. To most domestic manufacturers the profit margins for such small cars were not sufficiently attractive to justify a major production and marketing effort. Moreover, the relative importance of the small car market is countercyclical, that is, when the economy is growing and overall car sales are up, the small car share of the market is down. Conversely, when the economy is depressed, the small car share increases because sales of small fuel-efficient imported cars are less affected by declines in economic activity than are sales of large domestic cars.

What has happened since 1979 is that preference has shifted to small, fuel-efficient cars. The interesting thing about this shift is that it did not benefit only imported cars. Sales of smaller domestic models also increased as domestic manufacturers maintained their share of the small car market, despite the fact that their model offerings were limited.

What is happening in the market right now is that the depressed state of the economy is also discouraging car purchasers and the concern with fuel efficiency is intense as gasoline prices continue to rise. In this context, the inventory and production figures the question refers to can be understood. Chevettes and Citations must compete in a market with cars—imported and domestic—that have significantly better fuel-efficient and modern design, particularly front-wheel drive. The response to the K cars has been enthusiastic. While production may not be running as high as some would like, this is largely due to the depressed overall market.

Chevette, which incidentally was the largest selling model in the subcompact class in both 1979 and 1980, is a good example. Sales of Chevettes declined in December, and inventories rose. In January, however, Chevette sales were 34 percent above the December level; Datsun 210/310 models, which would be competitive with the Chevette, rose in January by 13 percent over December levels. While Chevette sales in January were approximately 18 percent below last year's levels, the Datsun 210/310 sales were about 39 percent below last year's levels.

Our point is that the domestic companies are competitive when and where they have the product. Clearly this has been demonstrated with Chevette and Citation. Mr. Secrest has pointed out that Escort/Lynx are selling at or near capacity.

The most obvious reason for Chrysler K cars to be doing not as well as expected is most likely attributable to three factors—Chrysler's initial pricing, the decision to produce mostly "loaded" cars at the start of the model year, and Chrysler's uncertain future (not many people want to buy a car that may become an "orphan"). Once Chrysler started producing less well equipped K cars, got their loan guarantee funds, and introduced rebates, K car sales have been very good, it seems to me.

Finally, it is worth noting that in today's market, purchasers appear to be very sensitive to price. If the success of the recent rebate programs are any indication, purchasers are resisting the significant price increases on domestic cars that have taken place over the last year.

Q: A car selling for $6,000 in the U.S. is said to cost $12,000 in Japan. What kinds of modifications must be made to our cars for sale in Japan? Are these modifications really justified or are they simply designed to price competition out of the Japanese domestic market?

SUZUKI: Every country, including the United States and Japan, has maintained the right to establish its own national standards for safety and pollution; and imported cars are required to comply with these standards. The difference between American and Japanese manufacturers is that Japanese manufacturers can make the changes required to comply with U.S. standards during their normal production process. By contrast, American manufacturers do not find it economical to adapt their production processes and, therefore, modifications to American cars to comply with Japanese regulations are done by hand once the cars reach Japan.

Modifications made in this manner can be expensive. It has been estimated in a report prepared by the U.S. General Accounting Office that such modifications (or homologation costs) cost from $110 per car for subcompacts to $535 per car for compacts.

While most Japanese standards are the equivalent of U.S. standards, it is true that because of greater population and vehicle density in Japan, requirements there tend to be more specific and more stringent. To actively facilitate the importation of autos, Japan has delayed the application of new environmental standards for the benefit of foreign manufacturers and sent government inspectors to the United States to expedite approvals. As a result, U.S. cars are generally approved for sale in Japan in no more than three months. U.S. approvals for Japanese cars to be sold in the United States take ten months.

In addition, consumers buying imported automobiles in Japan are generally affluent and demand that their cars be equipped with many features and gadgets. Another factor pushing up the modification cost is that Japanese consumers demand that cars be delivered in perfect finish and condition. It is not unusual, therefore for a Japanese dealer to have to realign door hinges and doors, to repaint an automobile to cover a scratch or two, or perform other necessary repairs on an imported car.

Q: Do the American manufacturers see any evidence that the Japanese have an edge in the engineering and design of their products?

SECREST: The engineering side of the business is not my specialty, but I don't see any evidence that the engineering of Japanese cars is superior to the engineering of American cars. I remember during the trade commission hearings this fall, the representatives of Nissan and Toyota pointed out that they had very few front-wheel drive cars (the Toyota model that is front-wheel drive has the engine the wrong way); to listen to my friends from the Japanese companies one would believe there was no evidence of engineering or design superiority.

On the other hand, the Japanese auto manufacturers do an excellent job, their products are very good, well-made and well-designed. I don't see any reason to believe that they are on the absolute leading edge of design, but maybe I don't know enough about it. I have heard that the Japanese nation has one-twentieth as many lawyers per capita as the United States, and considerably more engineers.

POTTER: I know of no inherent technical differences between our two countries' industries which give one an advantage over the other. But the application of various engineering technologies to auto production depends a bit on one's historical situation. When gasoline was 25 cents a gallon, the Chevrolet Caprice of the sixties was, in my opinion and in the view of many in the American public, a first-class well-optimized car. However, when gasoline prices are $1.50 - $2.00 a gallon, a different sized car becomes optimal, and that, of course, is the reason the U.S. auto industry has been rapidly moving to redesign its product lines. The Japanese and European importers have been optimizing the smaller car over a considerable period of time, and they have done a superb job, but there is nothing inherently lacking in our technology that keeps us from meeting this challenge.

Q: How can the absentee problems in the U.S. auto industry be reconciled with UAW goals to make the U.S. auto industry more competitive? What new approaches is the UAW prepared to take in order to deal with the absentee problem?

EPHLIN: The UAW established absentee committees at the Big Three in 1979 negotiations. We are working together jointly with Ford Motor Company trying several approaches to reducing absenteeism, including talking to employee groups through the Employee Involvement Program, explaining the cost of absenteeism.

Q: What can the UAW do to improve automotive quality?

EPHLIN: The UAW has initiated Employee Involvement programs with Ford Motor Company at many locations. Many of the programs are using Quality Control Circles. In addition, we have established an internal union reporting procedure for major quality problems so that we can call them to the attention of the company at the highest level.

Q: Please give some specific examples of opportunities to improve productivity without threatening job security.

EPHLIN: Quality improvement and the reduction of absenteeism actually improve productivity while at the same time improving the possibility of job security. We feel workers can make many positive contributions, all of which help to provide greater security.

Q: Does General Motors have any specific plans to give suppliers incentives to improve quality? How is this balanced against the price competition that seems to negate all other considerations?

POTTER: The incentive will certainly be that we are giving quality a heavier weight in the purchasing decision. When we evaluate a bid quoted by a supplier, we don't evaluate it on the basis of price alone. There are a number of important factors we consider. Quality is one of these, and it is receiving greater emphasis in our evaluations. As our new General Motors president, Jim McDonald, told a group of our suppliers last summer, "In the future we expect to pay more than the low price for quality products."

Q: Has Nissan adopted the "just-in-time" delivery system? If yes, how does it differ from the way it works at Toyota?

SUZUKI: Yes, Nissan has adopted a "just-in-time" delivery system called the Action Plate Method (APM). It is very similar in basic concepts to the Toyota system called the Kanban System. This very popular system has been explained in a published book on the subject.

Q: How can the problem of U.S. stockholder and management demands for short-term profits instead of long-term growth and gains be dealt with?

McCRACKEN: The major audience here ought to be financial analysts and the financial community. If they will start focusing more on the longer run, you can be sure that managements of U.S. corporations will respond. This is something that professors of business administration, economists, and spokesmen for the business community ought to stress more. Having said all of this, I do confess to a feeling that the point is sometimes overstated. I am a director of a few companies, and I certainly detect no lack of interest in where the company is going for the longer run in any of them.

Q: Is it only a matter of pressure from the IRS and regulatory agencies which impose short-term versus long-term expectations on the part of General Motors? Or do General Motors' policies and reward structures also promote such a short-term outlook?

POTTER: The issue of whether or not personnel policies and compensation programs inhibit the accomplishment of long-range objectives is one that is discussed with respect to almost every industry in the United States. Certainly compensation programs figure very importantly in a company's attention to long-range versus short-range goals, and this is an area where General Motors—and probably other U.S. companies—could give more emphasis. However, we believe General Motors' current commitment to a massive $40 billion capital investment program over the five-year period from 1980–1984 is a clear indication of our dedication to long-range objectives.

Q: In a recent article in the Harvard Business Review, Peter Drucker states that Japanese workers and their managers are not as cooperative as the U.S. press has indicated. He explains that the private sector unions are weak, and this makes a larger contribution to harmony than their collaborative management techniques that we've often heard about. Is this the case?

EPHLIN: If Japanese auto unions are weak, they are certainly not totally powerless; in recent years they have been increasing their benefits at a faster rate than we have. The J.A.W. resembles the U.A.W., and we have worked closely with the Japanese, assisting them in improving their bargaining techniques, and helping them strengthen their organization.

My experience, therefore, wouldn't lead me to say that harmony exists in Japanese labor-management relations because their unions are weak. I think the relationship is different for another reason: union reflects the management with whom they deal; everything in a union contract is there because of a problem that existed at some time, real or imaginary. The union movement in any country will be a mirror reflection of the management, and differences between Japanese and U.S. labor-management relations reflect differences in management traditions.

Q: What is your reaction to proposed legislation which would allow U.S. auto producers to get together to work on common problems without being threatened with violating anti-trust laws?

McCRACKEN: Unquestionably we in the United States, with our characteristic tendency in such matters, have carried matters of anti-trust into the theological zone. With the internationalization of the world economy, the scope and intensity of competition are enormously greater than used to be the case. My guess is that the major beneficiaries of our anti-trust laws have been members of the legal profession—not customers of our companies' products.

Q: Please comment on the relationship and support between the Japanese government and the auto industry. How do you think it differs from the United States?

SUZUKI: The Japanese auto industry receives no assistance, direct or indirect, of any kind from the government of Japan. Nor is Japan's automotive market protected by trade barriers; it is as (or more) open to imports as any other industrialized country.

It is true, historically, that Japan's auto industry did receive some measure of preferential treatment from the government. During the 1950s the auto industry, like some other industries in Japan, had preferred access to capital markets and to foreign exchange, and also shared in a broad tax stimulus program to promote high growth. Also during the 1950s and 1960s Japan did impose effective barriers to imports of motor vehicles and foreign investment. Japan had been devastated by World War II, and the process of industrial recovery required special measures. Today, ten to twenty years later, that history is of little relevance to understanding the controversy over U.S.-Japan trade in autos.

Japanese experience a certain frustration in hearing American protests about "Japan, Inc." First of all, it is in large part a myth. We also have aggressive regulatory agencies with which we must contend, and it was not too long ago that the Japanese auto industry successfully defeated government efforts to force mergers to reduce the number of auto manufacturers. On the other hand, probably because of the homgeneity of our culture and our perception that our resource-poor islands make our economic success quite vulnerable, Japanese in both industry and government have a sense that they share common problems and goals. From our point of view, however, this seems quite natural, and what appears to us extraordinary is the extent of adversary relationship that characterizes the interaction between business and government in the United States.

Q: Do you believe it is possible for the U.S. domestic auto producers to survive in the long run without merging or developing joint ventures with foreign manufacturers? Under such conditions what does it mean to have a national auto policy?

POTTER: I believe that it is possible. General Motors has never called for a "national auto policy," but has rather sought government policies that encourage the growth of business in general and help create a favorable climate for business investment.

Q: One of the key findings in the Department of Transportation's report released today is that there does seem to be a cost differential between the Japanese and American automobile industries, something in the neighborhood of $1,000 to $1,500 per unit. Is there any reasonable expectation that this differential can be narrowed?

BECKHAM: Having been burned a bit by predicting that the increased Japanese market penetration might be temporary, I want to be shy of making predictions. I will add, by the way, that I suggested that the Japanese consider voluntary restraints on imports in the same speech.

When we investigated the cost differential question in preparing the Department's report, we were able to break the difference into a number of components—differences in productivity, in the tax code, with anti-trust laws, and so on. Clearly if these specific components are dealt with, the position of the domestic auto industry will most likely improve.

Whether or not that happens depends partly on the industry's will to work on eliminating those differences, and partly on politics. The political side of the process is definitely advanced by the appearance of this report, in which the Department and the Secretary acknowledge and discuss ways of overcoming the Japanese cost advantage. We recognize the problem—and even Secretary Goldschmidt, from a part of the country where there is a significant foreign-car market—believes the problem needs to be rectified. I think we all now realize that if we wait three or five years to try to solve this problem, there may not be enough time to do it.

I might also add that in the present state of the car market, consumers in this country are very price conscious: price differentials, be they a thousand dollars or two hundred dollars, are enough to drive them from one car and one manufacturer to another. Consumers are able to postpone purchases and to shop for the lowest-priced car. There is considerable price resistance in the domestic market as a result, and that in itself is another piece of the current Japanese advantage.

SECREST: I'd like to add that although I guess I'd class myself as a relative alarmist and consider the situation facing the industry quite critical, I would not conclude that the Japanese cost advantage is so great that it cannot be substantially reduced or eliminated. Some of us can remember back around 1959 or 1960 when it seemed that the Germans were going to take over America with the amazing Volkswagen Beetle (with its long-ago-written-off tools), that the glorious German efficiency was going to just wipe us out. Now the Germans are coming here to produce, because their costs are as high as ours.

POTTER: I'm not an alarmist. We are going to narrow that differential, and we'll compete head on around the world.

EPHLIN: The U.A.W. would be happy to join with the auto companies, as Secretary Goldschmidt suggested, in an effort to eliminate the Japanese cost advantage by a combination of measures. I'm not volunteering any wage reductions—we don't think that would be productive. American auto workers buy automobiles, and unless someone can buy automobiles, all this production capacity isn't doing us much good. Auto workers enjoy high wages because the American auto industry has been the most productive industry in America for many years. But a pact such as Secretary Goldschmidt suggests, and the implementation of various kinds of trade restraints, and the fact that Japanese wage rates are currently increasing faster than American rates, all indicate that the gap can be narrowed. We think it can be done. As I mentioned, there are many other improvements that can be made—improved use of human resources, better management, and so forth—which can also help to decrease that difference.

SUZUKI: First, the Japanese have been accused of paying lower auto workers' wages for a long time. I tried to come up with some reasonable or fair wage comparison between Japan and U.S. auto workers. So far I haven't succeeded. However, back in 1978, the Labor Statistics Bureau came up with an auto worker wage figure comparison between Japan and this country. According to it, the American auto worker's wage per hour was $12.66 and the Japanese auto worker's hourly wage was $6.68; at this time, the average American production worker's wage was $6.17. Now we are talking about the cost advantage of the Japanese automobile; however, quite frankly speaking, I think it is very difficult for people who make $6.17 per hour to buy a car which is being made by a worker who earns $12.66 per hour. Therefore, I would really like to see the data from the Goldschmidt report which shows the big cost difference ranging from $1,000 to $1,500.

Q: One part of the U.S. productivity and technology problems might be the lack of programs in higher education that cultivate creative thinking processes; in fact, conformity seems to be encouraged. Are there changes in American colleges and universities that might address this problem?

POTTER: That's an allegation that has been made rather frequently. I do not subscribe to it to any significant degree. We get some very capable people from the major educational institutions in this country, some first-rate engineers and business people. I think everyone notes, however, a certain degree of conformity across the curricula in higher education that does not permit quite as much exploration of other course material that one would like to see. I would generally wish there were more broadly-based candidates for positions in our organization.

# THE LEGISLATIVE RESPONSE
## TO UNEMPLOYMENT IN THE AUTO INDUSTRY

Donald R. Riegle

Thank you very much. My colleague Senator Carl Levin, who was here earlier, and I both want to salute the efforts of the University of Michigan in organizing this conference and in attracting this tremendous and distinguished audience.

The report released yesterday by Secretary Goldschmidt, "The U.S. Automobile Industry in 1980," is in every repect a trailblazing effort. It shows a thoroughness and balance and objectivity and willingness to say say things that had to be said that makes it a refreshing example of the outstanding work public policy people from time to time can do. It addresses controversial and complex issues in groundbreaking ways.

The automotive industry in the United States is at a critical hour. Much of the data illustrating how serious our problems are was cited this morning: the fact that last year's automobile production was the lowest in nineteen years, that unemployment among auto workers and people in supplier industries is the worst seen since the great depression in this country, and that the auto industry's difficulties have added enormously to the federal deficit, both because of loss of taxable revenues on the income side and because of payments for unemployment compensation, trade adjustment assistance, food stamps, and other things on the expenditure side.

We are at a new point in our country's industrial history. Many lessons that were learned in other circumstances aren't particularly useful to us today; I think we in public policy positions and those of you in private sector positions have to resist the impulse to respond in ways that are suited to past problems. For many years we had a unique large-car market in the United States, profoundly different from any other market, since gasoline was cheap and easily available here.

All of a sudden things changed dramatically: from having small cars backed up in sales lots and big cars being hot ticket items to a situation where the large cars were no longer popular and it was the small cars that people wanted.

Everyone in this room knows (although a lot of people outside this room don't) that it takes at least five years for a complex industry of this size to redesign, reengineer, and rebuild both its product lines and its factories. And not only is it an expensive and difficult task for us (which we're now very much in the middle of doing), but also, in this larger world that we live in, we have some foreign competitors who were ideally positioned, having built small cars for a long time because of their market realities, to move into our market, and did so in record numbers. Twenty-seven-and-a-half percent of the U.S. domestic market last year was taken by foreign manufacturers, roughly twenty percent by the Japanese.

In understanding this new world market situation, we ought not to confuse it with the false notion that we have a free market. There is no free market in automobiles and there never has been. But the biggest market in the world happens to be a relatively free market, the one right here in America. Not surprisingly it is attractive to others, particularly to Japan.

I thought Fred Secrest made an excellent point earlier suggesting we might want to copy the Japanese example in certain respects, in production techniques or robotics or whatever; but we might also want to follow their example in closing off their domestic market while they built their modern automobile industry. Perhaps it's time for us to copy that part of their experience and protect our market. Japanese manufacturers sent 1.9 million cars into our country last year; the Japanese market took ten thousand of ours.

The urgency and size of the problem are plain: as we sit here there are meetings going on in Washington today in an effort to try to save the Chrysler Corporation, not exactly a small scale company by any means. We've also lost over two thousand automobile dealerships in the United States over the last couple of years. I talked with some auto dealers last night in Detroit at the Auto Show who said that time is running out for them, even those who have survived so far.

But even if we have one intelligent aspect of policy response, let's say in the trade area, or in changing the tax laws, I don't think we can begin to solve this problem unless we have the comprehensive strategy required. What I think the Goldschmidt report has done is to say this is a fundamental economic problem, affecting employment in the United States and the federal budget. But most importantly, the strength of our automotive industry influences our ability to mobilize for national defense. If we hope to be able to exercise leadership as a nation in the future, we can't do it from a weak internal economic situation.

Every other major country in the world has decided that a healthy industrial base is a national necessity; every other major nation in the world has backed the Japanese out by one means or another to make sure that its own domestic industrial base remained strong. Even today in West Germany, as the Japanese penetration of the West German market approaches 11 percent, pressures are building to restrain imports.

The Goldschmidt report calls for five-year import quotas to reduce Japanese penetration of our domestic market, until America has completed the changeover to small cars. David Potter of General Motors told me a few months ago that every tooling company in the world is booked to capacity right now just trying to handle the automobile industry changeover. So there are material restraints on how quickly this transition can be accomplished and that is why temporary quotas are necessary.

Another factor influencing the recovery of the U.S. auto industry is its need for adequate capital to cover the costs of this changeover. The 80 billion dollars earmarked by the industry won't be invested if it isn't available at affordable rates.

Automobile manufacturers in this country have not been shy in approaching the government for assistance: Chrysler Corporation asking for loan guarantees, and the Ford Motor Company for import restrictions to prevent further loss of sales to the Japanese. Chrysler's request for loan guarantees provoked a good deal of discussion, and the congressional decision to pass the necessary legislation followed an extensive investigation of the auto industry's future prospects. Not all the signs, frankly, are hopeful.

The Japanese advantage in productivity, which the Goldschmidt report estimates runs to $1000 - $1500 in cost per landed vehicle, is the principal indication of the U.S. industry's weakness. If the present situation continues, it seems unlikely that this differential advantage will be reduced. The best estimates are that something less than half of it is attributable to wage rate differential, and more than half to work process, robotics, newer capital, shorter transportation distances, and inventory advantages. Whatever its cause, reducing—and eventually eliminating—the Japanese cost advantage is the first challenge facing the U.S. automotive industry. Clearly many people in this room today will be responsible for meeting that challenge, and quickly.

Those of us on the public policy side are challenged to create conditions in which the capital the industry needs to work with is what it has to work with, to prevent counterproductive government intervention, and to foster cooperation among all sectors in responding to foreign competitors. But it seems clear that significant changes in the industry will be necessary to supplement changes in public policy: specifically changes in management and labor relations to promote a spirit of cooperation and a team effort in the work place at all levels. Changes are being made now, and there are many signs of improvement, but we've got to make major breakthroughs in this area, perhaps by following through on quality of work life programs or their equivalents.

The quality of industry-government relations in the United States is also open to improvement. I think the challenge we are facing today is in many respects like the challenge of World War II, when under great stress we were able to mobilize our people and industries to meet a national emergency. It so happens that the Japanese government cooperates extensively with Japanese industry, which has not been the pattern in the United States. In response to this new emergency, however, relations between the U.S. government and the auto industry have been changing: I think Neil Goldschmidt deserves credit for having done much to facilitate those changes.

But public policymakers also face pressures to ameliorate people-problems as well as industry problems. We're projecting employment level drops under the best of circumstances, and virtually catastrophic employment losses under the worst of circumstances. Many people and communities (especially in Michigan) will be affected no matter what happens, and we must have humane public policies in place to deal with that. We have not yet designed public policy programs that will handle a massive transition for the thousands of people who may be have to move out of an industrial sector that's being downsized permanently. That's an entirely new challenge. Not only don't we have the public policy mechanisms to deal with it, but we also haven't even started to debate them. The Presidential election campaign this last year didn't debate these issues.

The Senate Budget Committee did debate extending trade adjustment assistance benefits last year. I fought to increase the money earmarked for retraining, on the theory that many auto industry jobs might be disappearing permanently and that retraining might be most helpful to an unemployed auto worker. Everybody liked the idea, but nobody wanted to provide any money for it. So our present programs to aid displaced workers are inadequate.

Another aspect of government-auto industry relations, one that could stand improvement, is the way the two parties get along. I do not need to tell this audience what the auto industry thinks of official Washington. But it is worthwhile to point out that many people there, across both parties, have held negative opinions about the auto industry. Some believed simply that the industry was skirting its economic and civic responsibilities, not adapting to new markets and not giving U.S. consumers the best-quality product. Others, less critical, believed that the industry would fiercely and blindly resist any public policies regulating auto manufacture for the benefit of consumers. There has developed in some parts of Washington a contentious attitude towards the auto industry, which has been costly to the industry, to its workers, to our state and this region.

Some evidence that this may be changing would be the fact that we were able to get the Chrysler loan guarantee legislation through congress. I think five years ago the notion that any congress would have approved guaranteed loans for an automobile company would have been considered just implausible. But when we finally passed the Chrysler loan guarantee legislation on the last day of the session last year, any senator could have defeated the bill by merely prolonging debate. Although for many, voting against the Chrysler loan guarantee legislation would have been easier than voting for it, not a single senator was prepared to send the issue to the bottom at that time. And I think that's significant.

Official Washington is now prepared to help the automobile industry adjust itself to present and future conditions. The Senate Commerce Committee last year, as many of you know, recommended that adjustments in emissions standards designed to aid all American producers. Regulations requiring air bags have been dropped, and other executive and legislative regulations concerning manufacture and design have been modified. Changes in the tax laws are being proposed and debated. Trade restraints, such as Secretary Goldschmidt's report recommends, are a possible government response.

The idea of making the investment tax credit refundable will greatly help the auto industry. I am working on a refundability which would be workable and if realized would save the auto companies and suppliers billions of dollars when they most need it.

The policies of the Reagan administration are unknown at this point, but incoming transportation secretary Drew Lewis has said that he sees the problems of the auto industry as the most important issues facing the Department of Transportation, and that he will attempt to craft a broad policy response to them.

Auto industry problems are some of the toughest this country and its new president face.

We need programs capable of humanely and economically handling the widespread long-term unemployment workers in our industrial sectors are suffering.

We need to understand that if we treat auto industry problems as a business as usual situation, tough but manageable, then I think we're headed for disaster. Given the global scale of modern industry and its markets, I think it's conceivable that pressures could be exerted on the industrial base in the United States which could cut it in half. The auto industry and all its basic supplier industries may be facing a permanent downsizing.

The most reasonable response to this danger is to recognize some key initiatives that if taken together offer good prospects for restoring employment and maintaining industrial production. Some of these will be government actions. Some will clearly involve actions by management and labor to meet foreign competition and improve productivity. But to prevent the immense human problem that faces us in the worst case, these actions ought to be urgently and vigorously undertaken.

I say let's get on with the job.

Thank you.

# JAPANESE INDUSTRIAL POLICY:
## SOURCE OF STRENGTH FOR THE AUTOMOBILE INDUSTRY


Ira C. Magaziner


The Japanese government's industrial policy has contributed to Japan's overall industrial success and has played a formative role in the development of the Japanese automobile industry. This essay briefly describes this role and some of the general principles which govern Japanese industrial policy.


### Industrial Policy in Autos


The Japanese government created the Japanese automobile industry in the 1930s when for military and for foreign exchange reasons, it passed a law forcing the market leaders, General Motors and Ford, to leave Japan. After failing to encourage the large Japanese conglomerates (zaibatsu) to enter the industry, the government provided incentives for Toyota and Nissan to do so.

After the war, the government took the initiative to revive the industry. Toyota, the largest producer, was saved from bankruptcy in 1949 by the Bank of Japan. After this, the Japanese Ministry for International Trade and Industry (MITI) and the Bank of Japan disagreed on whether to promote an automobile industry. The bank felt it would divert too many resources from other uses, whereas MITI thought it was an essential industry for economic development. The Korean War resolved the issue by creating an export market for Japanese-produced cars. Beginning in 1952, MITI developed a policy to protect and help fund the development of the industry and to help it acquire needed technology.

The government played a significant role in the industry in the 1950s and 1960s. This role consisted of three major elements: early nurturing of the industry through protection and financing; attempts to rationalize industry production; and assistance with exports and overseas marketing and distribution.

MITI passed measures in the early 1950s which prohibited repatriation of earnings from marketing facilities of foreign automobile manufacturers in Japan and limited repatriation of profits on production facilities only to cases where they contributed to the development of the domestic industry. These laws were combined with quotas on imports in the 1950s and 1960s and prohibitively high tariffs which lasted through the early 1970s. MITI also extended direct reconstruction aid to the industry in the 1950s in the form of loans from the Japan Development Bank (a state bank), through special depreciation allowances and through direct grants to a technology development association representing the major manufacturers.

The purpose of these measures was to encourage the inflow of foreign expertise through joint venture and technology licenses, to protect the industry from foreign competition in its infancy and to provide seed capital to help revive the industry. These measures were generally successful in nurturing the industry's early development.

The second set of measures, those designed to rationalize the industry, had mixed success. These measures were aimed both at the auto parts industry as well as at the auto manufacturers themselves. For the auto parts industry, MITI initially aimed to consolidate the industry in order to create a group of large, specialized parts firms capable of competing with American suppliers. Long-term credit from the Japan Development Bank was extended to large suppliers from 1952 onward to assist their growth. In addition, between 1956 and 1966, a special committee representing MITI, the parts manufacturers, and the car manufacturers was established to administer a modernization and concentration program for the industry. Nearly $50 million in low interest long-term loans were extended over the period to support these efforts, and success was achieved. Market share concentration occurred, costs of production were reduced and automobile parts prices declined by roughly 30 percent per year between 1960 and 1965.

The concentrations which occurred during this period left a series of relatively efficient companies specializing in one or two parts. Between 1966 and 1971, MITI sponsored another program designed to encourage horizontal R & D cooperation and mergers to form large "unit system" sub assembly producers. MITI felt that such organizations would be stronger than the existing companies. Despite the offer of long-term, low-cost credit during a period of high growth and capital shortage, companies did not even fully utilize government budgets for this program. The major reason for the failure of this program was the attempts of the car makers, particularly Nissan and Toyota, to consolidate their own vertical linkages with component makers. These longstanding affiliations were tightened, thwarting government efforts at horizontal consolidation.

Thus, rationalization efforts of government played a significant role in promoting a competitive Japanes parts industry betwen 1956 and 1966, but MITI's thrust toward horizontal consolidation was not adopted by the industry in the late 1960s.

MITI's attempts to rationalize the car industry itself generally failed, however, though the process did exert some influence on producers. During the 1950s and 1960s, MITI attempted to consolidate the car industry into a few large groups in order to ensure a competitive industry when protection was inevitably ended in the early 1970s. Although MITI introduced various consolidation plans, the government and the manufacturers never achieved consensus.

In 1953, the Ministry rejected two of six applications for imports of foreign car technology, deeming the firms insufficiently strong to enter the car business. In 1955, MITI suggested that all car producers develop prototype "peoples cars" and allow MITI to select a winner which would then receive official backing. This idea was successfully resisted by the manufacturers. In 1961, MITI proposed that passenger car producers be organized into groups based on basic car design type. Three groups—regular passenger cars, mini-cars and specialty cars, including sports cars, were defined. A firm's entire production would be limited to one group, and minimum volumes would have to be met within three years. The objective was to force a concentration of product line and eventually eliminate small producers. Toyota and Nissan reportedly did not react negatively to the idea since they did not produce mini-cars and the plan would have reduced competition in conventional passenger cars. Toyo Kogyo, Mitsubishi, Daihatsu, and Fuji, on the other hand, all objected as they produced both mini-cars and conventional cars, and did not want to give up either business. Eventually, MITI's proposal was dropped.

In 1962, MITI tried again with a proposal for a comprehensive legislative charter to undertake, in cooperation with industry, major programs for promoting specialization, mergers, and groupings in selected industries, including automobiles. This law also failed.

Despite considerable financial inducements for mergers offered by the government, none took place until 1966 when Nissan and Prince merged and 1967 when Toyota associated with Hino and Daihatsu. The Japan Development Bank played a role in the first merger and also provided funding in support of the second. MITI, however, at the request of the manufacturers, played no role in the negotiations for the mergers.

At the end of the decade, it was clear that MITI's attempts to consolidate the industry had failed despite these mergers. MITI's legislative programs for consolidation had not been enacted, and its financial incentives for affiliation had drawn limited response.

The final group of measures were designed to promote Japanese exports by direct subsidy and by assistance for overseas marketing and distribution. Measures to subsidize exports have included export-import bank financing, plus a series of special tax incentives. Initially, a direct export income deduction could be taken by companies. After Japan joined GATT in 1964, this was discontinued and a series of less direct measures adopted. Under these measures, companies could establish tax-free reserves for overseas marketing development expenditures. Also, an accelerated depreciation schedule tied to export performance was initiated. The government also provided an export insurance program against default and helped set up a special parts center in Chicago in the mid-1960s to assist initial U.S. market penetration.

In general, these measures assisted development of export markets for Japanese automobile companies. They, as with all other selective measures related to the automobile industry, were dropped in the early 1970s once it was clear that the industry was fully competitive. Throughout the 1970s, the government played virtually no role in automobile industry development. From the point of view of government officials, there has been little need—the industry has been fully successful on its own.

More recently, two research projects are being supported by the government in Japan which are of assistance to automobile manufacturers; one focusing on the development of an electric car, and the other on general improvements in factory automation including multi-function robotics. The car industry is a partner in these projects along with companies from other Japanese industries.

One may speculate that MITI is also putting pressure on car companies to come to some accommodations with Western governments to reduce the risk of an automobile-induced war of protection against Japanese goods. Whatever the substance of the dialogue, there is little doubt that considerable strategic discussions are occurring between the companies and MITI on the subject.

Other than these activities, however, there is little government involvement in the automobile industry in Japan at the present time.

## General Influences of Industrial Policy

In addition to specific measures to promote the development of the automobile industry, some of the general principles which have attended the substance and process of industrial policy have provided a useful backup for all industry development in Japan.

The purpose of Japanese industrial policy is to raise the real income of the population by assisting the shift of resources to the applications in which they can be most productive. This is best accomplished by easing industrial transitions. Japanese policy is directed toward assisting the growth and competitiveness of infant industries and the phasing down of industries which can no longer be competitive in Japan due to raw materials disadvantages or changes in the international division of labor. Japanese industrial policy is benign in cases where companies are currently internationally competitive.

Japanese industrial policy is also attuned to the international competitive system—how competition varies by industry, and how the economies of businesses change over time. The role of Japanese government in industry varies by the place of the business in the international division of labor and by the competitive economic characteristics of the business. Government policy is flexible enough and government policymakers knowledgeable enough to respond to individual conditions within a given industry.

The conduct of Japanese industrial policy is relatively free of ideological debate. Generally, decisions are made on a pragmatic basis free from short-term political pressures and long-term debates on socialism versus capitalism or centralism versus populism. These debates shape overall political policy direction from the Diet, but not the conduct of day-to-day affairs.

Finally, the size of the bureaucracy and the amount of funds spent as part of Japanese industrial policy are both relatively small. The Japanese government has relatively few officials concerned with industrial policy and has not spent huge sums. It is, rather, the competence of the individuals and the wise use of resources which are crucial.

85

All of these aspects of the conduct of industrial policy have tended to create a stable, mutually reinforcing industrial climate between business and government. Though manufacturers and MITI have often not agreed, they have carried on a healthy dialogue based on common goals of enhancing Japanese competitiveness overall.

## Some Mythology

The foregoing description of Japanese industrial policy in general, and with respect to the automobile industry in particular, allows a number of myths about Japanese industrial policy to be dispelled.

The first myth is that of "Japan, Inc.," with the government orchestrating the whole industrial scene. As we have seen, the government certainly orchestrated the beginnings of the industry, but was highly unsuccessful in imposing its ideas on the automobile industry in the 1960s. Also, the government has played only a small role in the industry's development since the early 1970s.

A second myth is that, for cultural reasons, consensus comes easier among Japanese than among Americans. As we have seen, disagreements between MITI and various manufacturers were often left unresolved, and, on occasion, the only consensus reached was that no consensus was possible. Mergers of automakers which did take place were not done within MITI's influence, even though MITI had pushed for many years for them. Even within the government, disagreements on policy, such as that between the Bank of Japan and MITI over whether to revive the automobile industry after the war, are often resolved only by external events—in this case, the Korean war.

A third myth is that Japanese industrial policy is disappearing now that Japan has caught up to the West. Though, as we have shown, policies for the automobile industry declined in the 1970s, this is not totally indicative of trends in Japan in general. Certainly, Japanese industrial policy today cannot, and would not, use the same direct measures it did in the 1950s and early 1960s when it did not belong to GATT and was still recovering from the Second World War. However, active, selective policies to encourage the growth of knowledge–intensive industries where Japan is not yet a world leader (in areas such as electronics and industrial machinery), are being pursued—as are measures to assist structurally depressed industries. It would be a mistake for Western commentators to underestimate the sophistication of current Japanese industrial policy.

A final myth is to attribute too much primary influence in the success of Japan's automobile industry to government industrial policy. Though the activities described above played an important role, it has been the Japanese automobile companies—sometimes in opposition to government policy—who have been the crucial actors.

# QUALITY CONTROL PRACTICES IN THE AUTO INDUSTRY: UNITED STATES AND JAPAN COMPARED

Robert E. Cole

It is now clearly recognized by the public and the auto manufacturers that the quality of Japanese autos has significantly surpassed that of American cars.[*] Arguments over whether it is simply a matter of fit and finish (finish of sheet metal, paint, and accuracy with which parts fit together) are somewhat beside the point. A variety of studies, both proprietary and non-proprietary, consistently reveal a significant gap in the rate of mechanical failures reported by owners in the two nations' cars. Regardless of whether all these problems should be classified as fit and finish, there is growing recognition that problems of design, engineering, management, and assembly processes are involved.

To be sure, there are a number of bright spots for the American manufacturers in such areas as safety, corrosion resistance, structural integrity, and possibly durability of the power train. One might argue that if we compared all the various factors on which we can make quality measurements, the Americans might still be ahead on some overall measure. But this misses the point. The consumers have their own tally system and they are voting with their feet and dollars for the superior quality of Japanese imports. As we shall see in our discussion of the meaning of quality, their

* This paper draws heavily on information developed from extended interviews with and data collection from automotive officials in Japan and the United States. I would like to express my appreciation for their cooperation.

decision is the bottom line. It should be stressed, however, that contrary to the conventional wisdom, there is little evidence that American automotive quality has declined over the last decade. Rather, on measures of trouble frequency, for example, it is Japanese auto quality which has dramatically improved. These characteristics persist even adjusting for the relative "complexity" of the car.

These developments are especially difficult for U.S. auto firms because of a massive growth in quality consciousness among the car-buying public. Consumers appear to have a quality threshhold, the minimum acceptable level of which has been raised in recent years. And this level has been raised by the new standards established for the industry by the Japanese. This is not a bad position for them to be in: they have changed the "taste" of the consumer, and they are in a unique market position for satisfying that new "taste."

Until recently, product quality has not been given as much priority by U.S. auto firms as other considerations. Cost reduction, prompt delivery, and advancing overall production efficiency have often taken precedence over improved quality and reliability. This is changing as a result of massive pressures on the auto firms. These pressures come from the consumer movement, government regulation (including expanded product liability obligations), and above all the market pressures induced by the surge of high-quality Japanese products into the United States.

What do we mean by automotive quality? Quality is the entire collection of activities by which we achieve fitness for use as determined by the final user. This may be a matter of "peculiar" consumer taste, such as the way Japanese consumers demand tight-fitting doors, or it may involve the way a car fulfills its basic transportation function. By reliability, we mean simply the probability that the car will perform without failure—or more operationally, the mean time between failures.

It can be argued strongly that over the years U.S. auto manufacturers have been so busy competing with one another for profit maximization that they have not focused sufficiently on the fitness of their product as determined by the final user. To argue, as some auto people do, that we have a problem of consumer perceptions as opposed to "reality" is to miss the point entirely. The consumer definition of quality is reality.

Manufacturers followed Alfred Sloan's dictum, laid down in the 1920s, that in order to gain market share against a competitor it is not necessary to have greater than competitive quality. The result is that they tolerated significant amounts of scrap, bins of defective products, and the rework of defective products—along with an army of quality control inspectors and checkers and rework and repair personnel. This philosophy is symbolized by the acronym AQL. That is, U.S. auto firms aimed for an Acceptable Quality Level, in line with domestic competitors, and let the matter go at that. This philosophy stands in marked contrast to that of the Japanese auto firms, who are organized to attain continuous small-scale improvements—with the goal being elimination of defects. Moreover, the Japanese have successfully used high product quality as a major marketing strategy. Contrary to Sloan, they teach us that a quality superiority can be converted into higher price and/or market share.

What about some of the conventional explanations of the causes of relatively poor U.S. auto quality? A common view is that poor auto quality results from the decline of the so-called American work ethic.

Let me make three observations on this matter. First, as mentioned earlier, the trouble frequency of American cars has held steady over the last decade: it is the trouble frequency of Japanese cars which has rapidly declined. We can hardly attribute the Japanese improvements to a decline in the American work ethic!

Secondly, one often sees in American auto plants first-line supervisors who are under tremendous pressure from their general foremen to meet production quotas. And all too often, this leads them to order their subordinates to run substandard parts and let the final inspector or dealer worry about the problems that may create.

Thirdly, the poor quality (which the public attributes to poor workmanship) is often a function of poor training and inadequate job standards, not a lack of concern with quality on the part of workers. This is not to deny that high rates of absenteeism affect quality. They do, but they are only a relatively small part of the problem.

Poor quality is more a function of management priorities and reward systems than of a declining work ethic. All too often, employees at all levels of the organization get a gentle slap on the wrist for poor quality; but they get belted for failing to meet production quotas. Until some more balance in that reward equation is reached, all the management slogans, directives, and campaigns in the world will be ineffective in changing current practices.

So what is the explanation for the Japanese achievements? High product quality derives fundamentally from the application of specific management systems and strategies. We can better appreciate this point by looking at those organizational practices in Japan which have contributed to their moving to a position of world leadership in product quality. And we see these practices in industry after industry in Japan, not just in their auto firms.

I want to review three major areas: design engineering, vendor relations, and diffusion of quality responsibility.

Let me begin with engineering design. The greatest single source of field failures derives from weaknesses inherent in the design of a product. In Japanese manufacturing firms, the product design process is structured to build cooperative relationships with all those who will work with the design, including (especially) feedback from production workers. Loosely specified design drawings go through a long iterative process in which manufacturing staff, marketing, purchasing, sales, and quality control staff interact with the design personnel. Together, they gradually work out detailed specifications in a way which is satisfactory to all of them. Even vendors often become involved in this process. There is a support system for design engineers in which all parties take high product quality as a given. Quality personnel are armed with the authority to stop the release of a final design. This clout makes it less likely that quality and reliability will be seen as trade-offs for other priorities.

Once the product is in production, there is continuous feedback from manufacturing staff and production workers to engineering design—so that regular design modifications take place. In U.S. auto operations, one often comes across situations where, when a worker is confronted with out-of-tolerance parts, a decision will be made to run them without anyone making contact with engineering design. This contributes to a number of difficulties—among them being that the same problem may arise again and again.

In the United States, turf problems between design engineers and manufacturing staff are major issues. The assumption is that the engineering design department is relatively self-sufficient, possessing the skills and information necessary to meet the needs of product design. They tend to produce drawings which tell manufacturing exactly how they want the product to be made. Although arrangements for feedback from manufacturing are increasingly common, they are often highly formalized, less frequent than in Japanese firms, and occur later in the product design cycle. As a consequence, it becomes very difficult to change design specifications, and bureaucratic struggles between departments often result. Moreover, the pressures for shortening product cycle times (the period from product concept to production) are often so extreme that fitness for use gets downplayed, and final design approval is adjusted to conform to production schedules. This is despite the fact that one can pay with years of "production fixes" for not allowing enough time "up-front" in the product design phase. Finally, because U.S. quality personnel have commonly not had the authority to stop the release of engineering designs and have not reported to the highest levels in the corporation, they have been in a weak position to resist pressures to shorten product cycle time at the expense of quality.

Let me now move to a different set of factors. It is obvious that the quality of materials and components supplied by vendors (suppliers) strongly influences the quality of automobiles. In the United States, the value of purchased materials is estimated to account for 50 percent of the costs of auto manufacturing. The comparable figure for Japan is roughly 70 percent. Failure to improve the quality of vendor parts in the United States is a major factor in the quality gap between the U.S. and Japanese auto industries.

In the United States, vendors tend to be treated as independent parties. Their relationship with the auto firms is primarily contractual, with careful attention to the proprietary interests of the two parties. This often limits communication between the auto manufacturers and their vendors. The size of the staff devoted to vendor assistance in U.S. firms is miniscule, and contact with vendors (beyond inspection) tends to be limited to crisis situations.

Price competitiveness is usually the dominant criterion used in vendor selection. Vendors learn quickly to play the game, and quality is often sacrificed as a consequence. Manufacturers have difficulty tapping the innovative contributions of vendors. Vendors are seldom involved in the auto manufacturers' design processes.

The Japanese have evolved a quite different style. The relationship between vendor and buyer is more one of interdependence rather than independence. Strenuous efforts are made to have the vendor, in cooperation with the auto manufacturer, insure product quality beforehand. Vendor selection involves not only examining production samples, as is the general practice in the United States, but also assessing the actual process capability of the vendor. Above all, vendor relations are based on systematic and continuing exchanges of information and services along three dimensions: technological, economic, and managerial. Indeed, some Japanese automakers and partsmakers jointly own research facilities. Exchanges between the auto firms and partsmakers involve extensive mutual visting of each other's work sites. Monthly meetings with vendors are normal operating procedure, and there is a large management staff devoted to working with vendors. There is less stress on maintaining proprietary interests; vendors tend not to supply rivals, so this is less of a problem in Japan. While price competitiveness is a most important consideration in selecting vendors, great stress is also placed on vendor loyalty, quality, and dependability.

A third area of investigation lies in the organization of quality control operations. In the Japanese model, the major responsibility for quality assurance is placed on the line managers and production employees with minimal use of staff specialists. Extensive company-wide training in quality control exists, from top management down to and including production workers.

A word about production workers' involvement is in order. Through quality control circles and similar small group participative activities, production workers receive training in quality control and learn to identify and solve workshop problems. They engage in a great deal of self-inspection and routine machine maintenance. At Toyota they are equipped with line stop buttons which they can use without prior consultation with superiors—hard to imagine that in a U.S. auto firm. This line stop system helps pinpoint accurately the exact location and potential cause of quality problems.

All these arrangements to involve workers in quality must be understood in a broader context. Japanese managers treat their employees as resources which if cultivated will yield economic returns to the firm. That means you invest in training for all employees; great stress is placed on developing a multi-skilled labor force cross-trained in a number of jobs. All workers are seen as capable and desirous of making contributions to the firm. Japanese auto production workers are on monthly salary; they are made to feel like fully contributing members of the firm.

By comparison, the model operative in U.S. auto firms presumes a separate and large staff of quality specialists from inspectors to quality control and reliability engineers. These individuals are expected to take major responsibility for achieving quality. The advantages of this approach are not to be underestimated. But there are some costs—which are being increasingly recognized. The system does not fully utilize all the firm's available human resources. As one senior U.S. auto executive said to me: "We wrote off the workers as contributors to the organization in the 1930s when they unionized."

At another level, consider that U.S. auto assembly plants report a ratio of one full-time inspector for every twenty production workers. The ratio for Toyota is one full-time inspector for every thirty production workers. That is a significant cost savings for the Japanese that shows up as increased productivity. The reliance on inspectors in the United States leads hourly personnel to be lax about work standards, since they know someone else will fix the problem. This leads management to hire more inspectors, and workers become even more lax. Indeed, the problems are often passed on to the dealer, who is provided with "dealer preparation" fees to make final adjustments and corrections. This positive feedback loop is extraordinarily detrimental to product quality and has severe cost consequences. In Japan, doing the job right the first time and building quality into the product are more than slogans. They are built into the structure of the organization. Reliance on worker self-inspection encourages attention to detail and preventive problem-solving, and reduces the overhead costs of hiring full-time inspectors.

The most publicized Japanese innovation in quality control is the effort to have production employees take greater responsibility for quality through the development of quality circles, where they learn to identify and solve workshop problems, using simple statistical problem-solving techniques. All the major auto firms carry out large-scale small group participatory activities of this nature. At Toyota, for example, with a total of 47,000 employees, there are 4,200 quality control circles involving almost all production workers. To give you an impression of the significance of these activities, let me note the following: General Motors is generating on the average .84 suggestions per eligible employee per year, with about 22 percent of these suggestions being adopted. In 1980, Toyota Motor reports generating 17.8 suggestions per employee per year—and more importantly, about 90 percent of these suggestions are adopted. This means that not only are they getting more suggestions (20 times as many), but they are also getting better ones. Nor are these figures unusual for both U.S. and Japanese industries. For those who assume these differences derive from cultural differences, it should be stressed that ten years ago, Toyota was generating very few suggestions, and they had a much lower adoption rate. There has been a rapid rise in the number of employee suggestions in Japanese auto firms over the last decade. One cannot help but note the high correlation with the rapid increase in Japanese auto quality.

In conclusion, the sources of the growing Japanese advantage in auto quality are varied. Central to the strategy adopted by the Japanese is a strong effort to get all employees to take responsibility for improved quality. Secondly, the Japanese have recognized that quality and productivity are not contradictory objectives but mutually supportive ones. Thirdly, the Japanese recognize that quality is a carrier for other desirable corporate objectives such as employee involvement in decision-making, inventory control, increased market share, and of course productivity.

The pressures on U.S. auto firms to upgrade quality are intense, and some significant movement is apparent. Let me note just a few of the directions being taken:

1) More authority is being given to quality control personnel, and they are reporting to higher levels in the organization. This gives added prominence and clout to the quality assurance effort.

2) At many plants across the country, union and management people are sitting down and discussing the possibilities for cooperative activity in upgrading quality.

3) A great deal of publicity is being given to the new quality campaigns within all the major auto firms and suppliers.

4) Efforts are being made to improve coordination between engineering and manufacturing. I think particularly of the efforts at the Chevrolet Flint engine plant which is building the L-4 1.8 liter engine for the J-car. They are actually trying to "build the engine to print."

5) Greater attention is being paid to vendor quality.

6) Perhaps the most visible is the extensive experimentation going on with quality control circles. General Motors estimates that some 12 plants are now experimenting with the circles and a variety of other participative activities are occurring as well; Ford Motor Company is also moving rapidly ahead in this area. The UAW has been very much involved in these efforts.

Are these various developments portents of a basic change in the future as David Potter asserts? I am not as sanguine about the outcome as he appears to be.

There is a lot of pressure for instant solutions, and management may not have the patience to continue with efforts which don't yield immediate results. The quality control circles are a case in point. In Japan, they emerged as a final stage of the attempt to upgrade quality. But many U.S. firms are jumping right into circles without much preparation and without much recognition of what else has to change before the circles can really make a contribution. In that situation, there are going to be a lot of failures.

In one sense, we can reduce the whole Japanese approach to a matter of cooperation. Manufacturing cooperates with engineering design, the auto firms cooperate with the vendors, and management cooperates with its labor force. That is a rather simplistic formulation, but it does capture a general aspect of the Japanese approach.

Is the cooperative model, however, one which we can emulate? We have a set of practices built up to a greater extent on an adversarial model. And while it is all the fashion to say that we have to do away with adversarial relationships, I think they contribute some real strengths. After all, we didn't arrive at our position of world leadership in the automobile industry by doing everything wrong. As David Potter notes, it may be a matter of building on existing practices and adapting Japanese practices to our own environment, just as they adapted our practices to their environment.

This is not to say that we can't build a little more cooperation into the system. One place for us to start is with our reward systems. Do we reward our vendors primarily for price, or do we also evaluate highly product quality? Do we reward workers simply for following orders, or do we start to reward them for using their brains? Do we reward manufacturing staff exclusively for meeting production quotas, or do we also reward them for things like feeding back information to engineering design?

There are a lot of obstacles to moving forward in the area of quality. But we have only the choice of going forward or watching our competitive position erode still further. Meanwhile the Japanese are hardly standing still and waiting for the United States to catch up. They are hard at work in search of future quality breakthroughs in such areas as design, dealer service, maintainability, and especially consumer education in quality.

# ANALYSIS OF U.S. AND JAPANESE
# AUTOMOTIVE TECHNOLOGY

## David E. Cole

While the U.S. automotive industry is in the midst of its most severe trial in 50 years, the Japanese industry is thriving, growing at an unprecedented rate, and expanding its position in markets throughout the world. Last year, for the first time, Japan became the world's number one producer of passenger cars. Nowhere else is Japanese automotive success more evident than in the United States.

We are looking for the key factors in this significant shift to Japanese vehicles and the relatively poor performance of domestic models in the U.S. market. Is technology a factor? Can the U.S. automotive industry reverse the trend? Will sales of U.S.-produced cars continue at the depressed level of the past two years? What will be the long-term impact of poor sales on the U.S. auto manufacturers, their suppliers and employees, and on the consumer, and local, state and national governments? These are difficult questions with complex answers, if answers exist at all.

My remarks are intended to contribute to a better understanding of the Japanese automotive challenge from a technological perspective. Foremost in importance among all technological aspects of the automotive industry, whether here or in Japan or elsewhere, is the long lead time required to make major product changes. Many of the problems facing the U.S. automotive industry stem directly from long lead times and consequent inability to meet rapidly gyrating customer demand. If automotive vehicle manufac-

99

turers could change their basic product offerings instantly, we would probably not be meeting here today. An intelligent grasp of these lead time requirements is a prerequisite to understanding automotive developments in the United States during the last several years.

The process leading to the production in high volume of a new product line with new bodies, new engines, and new transmissions, must begin four to five years before the first production model rolls off the assembly line. For example, shortly after the blow-up in Iran in early 1979, General Motors introduced its instantly popular "X" cars. To the uninformed this seemed to be a clever, fast-moving reaction on the part of General Motors. In fact, however, the initial planning for the X car program was started in the fall of 1973, over five years before the Iranian crisis.

In order for a company the size of General Motors, Ford, or Chrysler to revise all of its product lines, at least seven years are required. To add major new facilities to produce a substantially increased volume of an existing vehicle that is already in production can take two years or more.

The major factors behind these lengthy lead times are the limited availability of personnel, capital, and machine tool manufacturing facilities. If this discussion leaves you with the feeling that the automotive industry moves a little slowly, consider the following comparison: it required a $25 billion investment and took 10 years to put a man on the moon; the U.S. automotive industry, including its suppliers, is in the midst of a program to invest $125 billion in five years—five times as much in half the time.

Before starting the technical analysis, I want to point out that the U.S. passenger car market must be kept in perspective. We must remember the breadth of consumer needs and the cyclical environment in which the automotive industry operates. It should not be assumed that nothing but jewel-like small cars will ever again be bought.

The upswing in the small car share of the market has moved too far too fast to be sustained unless there is a substantial permanent decrease in oil imports. Many families need a good sized car to carry the family and their luggage.

If, as now seems possible, the federal government allows more reliance on free market forces, we could see a strong comeback for family sized cars.

## The U.S. Automotive Industry Situation

Lead-time limitations played a major role in the sequence of events culminating in the existing problems of the American automotive industry. Many people hold the erroneous belief that the U.S. industry met its fate because of poor management and inadequate planning. But the chronological facts point, at least in part, in a different direction.

In 1973 we had Oil Shock I. World oil prices rose rapidly, government misallocations of fuel caused long lines to appear at service stations, and there was a panic rush to buy small cars. No manufacturer was prepared to meet the sudden demand for small cars in early 1974. Toyota, Datsun, and Volkswagen ran just as short as U.S. manufacturers. All U.S. manufacturers announced major plans to expand small car production.

But, in the spring of 1974, with gasoline still under government price control at 55 cents per gallon, the small car buying panic leveled off. There was a measurable trend back to larger cars. By the summer and fall of 1974, imports were barely holding their own; domestic small cars were a glut on the market.

In early 1975 the President's office proposed that price controls on oil and gasoline be quickly phased out; the U.S. automotive companies were 100 percent in favor of this plan. They were anxious to get their customers back to reality so that the market place would give valid product preference signals. The companies all knew that fuel-efficient cars were the wave of the future, and they were becoming increasingly concerned that the longer the wave was delayed the more difficult it would be to judge its timing and the more likely it would arrive as an overwhelmingly destructive tidal wave.

However, by mid–1975, little over a year after Oil Shock I, the U.S. Congress and the U.S. media had convinced each other and the public that there really never had been an oil problem in 1973—it had all been an oil company hoax. Congress acted to <u>reduce</u> the ceiling prices on oil and gasoline under the Energy Policy and Conservation Act of 1975. Recognizing that reduced prices might not actually lead to conservation, the Act also required the U.S. automotive companies to meet a series of increasingly more stringent corporate average fuel economy (CAFE) standards.

Government policy makers gave lip service to energy conservation but their pricing actions spoke otherwise to unsophisticated consumers who apparently believed, judging by their actions, that gasoline would always be cheap and available. Much of the buying public went back to its first love—large, powerful, comfortable, safe passenger cars—and discovered multiple new romances with vans and pickup trucks and recreational vehicles.

A "big car binge" began and did not stop until Oil Shock II occurred when a revolutionary government came to power in Iran.

During all this market exuberance, the U.S. automotive industry was trying to plan to meet CAFE requirements. Did they dare make the huge investments necessary to meet CAFE standards when they knew that if enough buyers complained about being forced to buy small cars, Congress could reverse itself, could reduce billions of dollars of small-car facilities to scrap?

Import sales were holding their own at record high levels around 15-18 percent of market, but what did that prove? With their high volume requirements, any big-three domestic producer that had made an early enough total commitment to small cars to introduce them before 1979 would have been out of business before it could reap rewards following Oil Shock II in early 1979.

U.S. automotive manufacturers are striving to reduce their

lead-times and achieving some success but a breakthrough to a significant reduction in lead times is not probable.

They are also improving their manufacturing flexibility to increase their ability to change vehicle production facilities to meet sudden shifts in buyer demand. But there are severe financial limitations to flexibility; no company can afford to maintain large amounts of idle capital equipment on the off chance that it may be needed at some unknown time in the future. A company operating profitably at a given share of market cannot possibly maintain enough idle capital equipment to be able to get the same share of market if buyer demand changes overnight from large cars to small, or vice versa.

### The Japanese Automotive Story: Fact and Fiction

Within a society, individuals and groups differ, of course, but Japan, in contrast to the United States, is a homogeneous nation untroubled by most of our divisive issues, and with industry, labor, and government jointly dedicated to the common goal of increasing industrial productivity and improving quality. The result of this three-way cooperation and concentrated dedication is an increasing flood of high-quality competitively priced industrial and consumer products that have put Japan in third place in the world, behind the United States and the Soviet Union.

Because of its limited resources and need to export, Japan must make maximum use of science, engineering, and technology, and avoid self-destructive adversarial relationships. On a per capita basis, the United States has only half as many engineers as Japan and over 83 times as many lawyers.

We cannot legislate or collectively bargain for the Japanese work ethic or spirit of cooperation, but we can look for strong points that might apply here. We should respect the Japanese for their many accomplishments but not attribute too much to them. Keep in mind that Japan is oriented to miniaturization—a compact society, with people small in stature, limited resources, and limited choices. Local circumstances forced Japanese manufacturers to produce small, efficient passenger cars and thereby also forced them to learn how to make small vehicles as attractive as possible.

When outside influences finally forced U.S. car buyers to think small, the Japanese cars were available because they were sold in volume at home. If Japanese manufacturers had attempted to capture their present high share of the U.S. market without domestic sales and cost advantages to support them, it is highly doubtful that they would have succeeded.

It is widely believed that the general level of Japanese technology is ahead of ours, but this is not true. Generally, I believe U.S. industrial technology is several years ahead of Japan and will increase this advantage if our industry is successful in its plans over the next five years. It is true that the Japanese have a high proportion of the relatively few industrial robots in operation world-wide, but robots currently account for only a small fraction of production in Japan and elsewhere. We should not be complacent about our technological lead over Japan; we need every bit of it and more because the Japanese are currently winning the competitive battle.

Japanese vehicle manufacturers are strong on development and aggressively implement new technology even if "not invented there." Part of their aggressiveness reflects their government's willingness to back them up financially and allow them to pool resources in joint development projects. Furthermore, they can count on highly supportive, flexible cooperation from their labor force.

Examples of appropriated technology include the Honda CVCC stratified charge engine, invented in England 60 years ago, and the rotary engine, invented in Germany. The rotary engine has been developed by Japanese manufacturers to a point of competing with the fuel-efficiency of conventional piston engines.

Now Japan faces the necessity of leading the way in creating new energy and material technologies because these costs are accelerating much faster than others. Whether the Japanese can be technically inventive, as well as innovative, remains to be seen.

Japanese productivity has improved rapidly and substantially, but the United States remains the overall productivity champ— although by a decreasing margin. In 1979, according to government figures, the average Japanese worker produced 66 percent as much as the average American, compared to 55 percent six years earlier. It is not clear whether the Japanese automotive industry is more or less productive than ours but they are close either way.

Productivity growth rates are a clear-cut story—Japan ranks number one and the United States a lowly seventh place. In recent years, Japan's annual productivity improvement has been over three times that in the United States.

There are few questions among those technically literate about the reason for our lag in productivity improvements. It is caused by federal government laws and regulations that favor nonproductive goals.

Quoting from the November 14, 1980, issue of Science:

> Government policies affecting industry—tax, trade, tariff, regulatory, and so on—are generally better coordinated in Japan than they are in the United States. The overall approach is regarded by some observers as more pragmatic and less ruled by abstract principles. For instance, U.S. antitrust laws would prohibit much of the kind of business collaboration that in Japan is regarded as necessary to ensure the health of a whole sector.

Key elements in the Japanese success story are:

1) Emphasis on quality from design through post-delivery service.
2) Productivity through high efficiency rather than high cycle rate.
3) Well-educated, technically literate, bureaucrats and workers.

4) Constructive and progressive worker attitudes.
5) Union flexibility.
6) Supportive, nonpunitive government.

## Technological Trends

Recently I participated in the design and management of a major survey of technical, marketing, and administrative decision makers in the automotive and supplier industry. We developed a consensus view of the automotive future.

Automotive engines of the future will be predominantly in-line 4-cylinder and V-6 designs. In 1990 the 4-cylinder production may be as high as 75 percent.

More exotic engine concepts such as the gas turbine or the Stirling engine are not expected in the 1980s.

The front-engine, front-drive concept with the engine located transversely in the vehicle will become the predominant passenger car drive train. The conversion to new engines and drive trains will be enormously expensive.

Electronics are expected to play an increasingly prominent role.

In general, lightweight materials will come into far greater use in the never ending drive of the automotive designer to maintain the largest possible passenger and load volume while reducing vehicle weight to minimize fuel consumption. The average weight of the U.S. produced car should drop from 3300 pounds in 1980 to 2900 pounds in 1985 and finally to 2500 pounds in 1990. Steel and cast-iron use will be reduced significantly. At the same time, the use of aluminum and of plastic in all its various forms will expand dramatically.

## Quality

"Quality" can mean just about whatever a customer thinks or wants it to mean. One of our objectives here is to clarify the issue.

A recent survey reported that Americans perceive Japanese cars to have better overall quality than U.S. cars. This viewpoint may be widely held in the United States. However, we are not convinced that the quality of Japanese cars is superior to U.S. built cars on an overall basis.

We believe that "quality" refers to the fitness for use of the entire vehicle and not just to surface appearance. Quality should be broadly defined to include consumer value items other than the readily perceived fit and finish factors. Total quality is a consideration in total value received by customers. Total quality has many facets, including fit and finish, but also, and more importantly, durability, structural integrity, repair cost, maintenance requirements, fuel economy, performance, corrosion resistance, size, weight, roominess, comfort, styling, and highway safety. Many of these more important quality factors are hidden and not apparent to the typical, non-technical, customer.

It is extremely important to remember when comparing the quality of U.S. cars to imports that U.S. quality has continued to improve steadily and is at high levels; imported car quality advantages, such as they are, have come from import improvements, not from a failure to progress here. Well before Japanese cars became popular in America, U.S. manufacturers had demonstrated their ability to improve quality. How long has it been since you had to change the oil in your car every thousand miles? Scheduled maintenance on a 1971 Dodge Dart would have cost a total of $760 for five years at today's prices; the cost for a 1981 Chrysler "K" car would be $160. Thirty years ago it was headline news in Popular Mechanics magazine when a car went 100,000 miles without a major engine overhaul; now we expect this as a matter of course.

Import quality has improved rapidly because it had a lot of catching up to do. Ten years ago, imported cars represented 15 percent of U.S. sales but accounted for 70 percent of recalls. One could believe, based on the present enthusiasm, that Japanese products have always been excellent but only now are receiving their rightful recognition. The truth is, the high level of Japanese quality is recent and as little as 10 years ago the typical Japanese automobile was not a competitive product; it was inferior in most measures we use to judge automobiles. They have made remarkable progress in a short time.

With a comprehensive definition of quality in mind, I want to draw technical comparisons between U.S. and Japanese automotive products. I must speak largely in generalities, with the use of some examples, because it is not practical to construct weighted average ratings for all Japanese and U.S. cars. Further, some of the comparisons require value judgments that are at least partially subjective.

## Fit and Finish

I believe that Japanese cars have excellent fit and finish quality that is generally better than that of U.S. products. However, based on personal inspection of recent vehicles, the differences are modest and being reduced.

Fit and finish I have labeled "perceived quality." Clearly, Japanese cars are excellent in this regard. The doors fit well and close easily. Misalignment of body panels is rare. The trim is installed properly and body finish is superb. The Japanese have placed special emphasis on this category of quality—their success is evident. They have come a long way in a comparatively short time because a true team spirit exists between management and labor. In part the Japanese culture and national resolve to be successful in the world's marketplace have lead to their commitment to perceived quality. This program is strengthened by the Japanese preoccupation with fine detail so evident in all forms of their technology, art, and general life style.

The fit and finish of U.S. vehicles is good but not equivalent to the Japanese on the average. We have not placed as much emphasis on it in design and manufacturing at all levels from management to the hourly laborer. In part this lack of emphasis reflects the fact that the U.S. market was not in the past "tuned" to details of fit and finish. Emphasis was on power, size, durability, or other consumer factors. Some experts state that U.S. surface finishes are actually more durable than the Japanese although perhaps not as well applied.

The technical and managerial requirements to match the Japanese level of fit and finish are well understood by the U.S. industry. In Europe, where customers demand a level of fit and finish quality equivalent to the Japanese standard, General Motors and Ford have about the same share of market that Japanese cars get in the United States.

Another factor in fit and finish comparisons is the American preoccupation with diversity. In years past, U.S. manufacturers have made it possible to build literally thousands of cars, all different from one another by virtue of a wide selection of exterior colors, interior and exterior trim packages, and a multitude of accessories and options. In contrast, the Japanese concentrate on perfecting the appearance of a much smaller range of offerings.

The U.S. manufacturers have made dramatic progress in the past several years to improve their perceived quality, and I would urge each of you to make a personal inspection of current U.S. produced vehicles. Do not rely on hearsay and conjecture; look and compare. I think you will find great improvements but still not parity with the Japanese. I predict, however, that within three years the U.S. made vehicles will match their Japanese counterparts.

## Structural Integrity

The structural integrity of the latest American vehicles is outstanding. Advanced computer-aided design techniques and experience developed over the years have led to highly efficient structures. They are rigid and strong, with frontal structures that are efficient absorbers of energy (which is so important in a frontal impact crash) and light weight for the volume contained. Even with the shift from separate body-frame to integral body-frame design, my judgment is that the basic structure of U.S. vehicles is as at least equivalent and perhaps superior to Japanese vehicles.

I wish each of you could have the opportunity to witness the use of computer aided design technology developed in the Aerospace industry and advanced by the automotive companies and their suppliers. We are rapidly approaching true optimization of automotive structures while at the same time decreasing the lead time from concept to production. Based on my own review of the literature and personal discussions it is my impression that the United States is ahead of all international competition in this area.

## Ride, Handling, Comfort

Ride, handling, comfort—few performance factors in the automobile are as subjective as these. What is "good for the goose is often not good for the gander." It is impossible to design one vehicle to satisfy the expectations of all customers. The sporty set likes a more rigid sharp ride which is consistent with crisp handling whereas the comfort lovers are more interested in flat, low frequency ride motions with predictable but not necessarily high performance handling. Comfort includes ride and handling and also temperature control, wind and structural noise, and vibration. These latter factors while partly subjective are more easily quantified, and there is general agreement on standards.

Japanese and American vehicles are excellent with regard to all of these parameters in my opinion. Modern large and midsize American vehicles with separate body-frame design are truly extraordinary from an overall ride and comfort standpoint and at least the equal of any car in the world, no matter the price. Certainly they are superior to the generally smaller uni-body

Japanese cars. The new integral body frame U.S. cars, while lacking the additional layer of vibration isolation between the body and frame, have proven to be nearly the equal of their larger brothers and again, in my opinion, appear to offer greater comfort and at least comparable ride and handling to the Japanese products.

Specific comfort items that I have observed differences in include heaters and air conditioning systems with general superiority in U.S. cars and greater quietness in U.S. cars in both wind and chassis noise. The Japanese standard seats are generally better than the base U.S. configuration. Again, I must emphasize the subjective nature of many of these evaluations.

Fuel Economy

In this day of energy concern, fuel efficiency has never been more important in our motor vehicles. The average new Japanese car is considerably better than the average new U.S. car although on a percentage basis U.S. cars have been greatly improved by the downsizing and redesign efforts of the past several years. The major factors in the Japanese efficiency lead are their smaller size and lighter weight plus the availability of features such as 5-speed transmissions.

To develop a valid yardstick for comparing Japanese and U.S. technology, it is necessary to normalize with respect to key parameters. I think an appropriate factor is total interior volume. For our purposes I have used EPA combined passenger and luggage volume and urban fuel economy data. Comparison should be with an equivalent transmission and engine type. It would also be useful to generate an equal performance normalization but this is very difficult with the data at hand. For these calculations I have converted efficiency performance to gallons/mile rather than miles/gallon. The normalized data are thus expressed as gallons/mile per cubic foot of total interior volume. Results for representative passenger cars are shown in Table 1. As in golf, the lower the score the better the performance.

TABLE 1
1981 Representative Fuel Consumption Comparison:
Japanese vs. U.S. Cars
(automatic transmissions, smallest engine available)

| Car Model | No. of Pass. | Total EPA Int. Volume | EPA Urban MPG | Combined Fuel Economy—Volume Ratings | |
|---|---|---|---|---|---|
| | | | | Gal./Mile/ Cu.Ft. | Gal./Mile/ Passenger |
| GM Chevette Hatchback | 4 | 89 | 26 | $4.3 \times 10^{-4}$ | $9.6 \times 10^{-3}$ |
| GM "X" Car Hatchback | 5 | 115 | 23 | 3.7 | 8.6 |
| GM Chevrolet 4 Dr. Malibu | 6 | 119 | 19 | 4.4 | 8.7 |
| GM Chevrolet 4 Dr. Caprice | 6 | 131 | 19 | 4.0 | 8.7 |
| Ford Fairmont 4 Dr. | 6 | 113 | 22 | 4.0 | 7.6 |
| Ford LTD 4 Dr. | 6 | 133 | 16 | 4.6 | 10.4 |
| Chrysler "K" Car | 5/6 | 110 | 24 | 3.8 | 6.9 |
| Honda Civic Hatchback | 4 | 82 | 29 | 4.2 | 8.6 |
| Honda Prelude 2 Dr. | 4 | 81 | 24 | 5.1 | 10.4 |
| Honda Accord 4 Dr. | 4 | 91 | 24 | 4.5 | 10.4 |
| Datsun 210 Hatchback | 4 | 85 | 29 | 4.0 | 8.6 |
| Datsun 510 Hatchback | 4 | 87 | 27 | 4.2 | 9.3 |
| Toyota Celica Hatchback | 4 | 89 | 25 | 4.5 | 10.0 |
| Toyota Corolla Hatchback | 4 | 89 | 27 | 4.2 | 9.2 |
| Toyota Tercel Hatchback | 4 | 93 | 29 | 3.7 | 8.6 |

Note, in the second-to-last column, that the best rating of 3.7 is shared by a relatively large, mid-sized hatchback GM "X" car, and the two-classes smaller subcompact Toyota Tercel. The Chrysler "K" car at 3.8 is almost equal to the 3.7 Tercel and better than the other seven Japanese cars listed. The Ford Fairmont, at 4.0, is equal to or better than all the Japanese cars except the Tercel. The Chevrolet Caprice, classified by EPA as a large car, rates better than most Japanese cars.

These combined fuel economy-volume ratings are not an attempt to downgrade the importance of fuel-economy, but to put it into perspective and to demonstrate that U.S. automotive technology is equivalent to or superior to that of Japan when the total vehicle is considered.

## Performance

Performance includes the traditional considerations of off-the-line acceleration and passing ability and, in addition, the capacity to perform chores such as pulling a boat or a house trailer. No large advantages accrue to either American or Japanese vehicles of a comparable size but only a full sized car can meet full size towing requirements, and there are no large Japanese passenger cars.

## Repair and Maintenance

Not many years ago, passenger cars required periodic service every 1,000 miles. Today the interval is 6,000 to 8,000 miles. It will be 10,000 miles on 1985 model cars and 15,000 in 1990. U.S. passenger cars have the lead here and the Japanese and others are following. The U.S. automotive industry pioneered the mass-produced electronic ignition, long intervals between oil and spark plug changes, and other service advantages. U.S. cars are less expensive than Japanese cars with respect to regularly scheduled maintenance.

There has been remarkable general progress in preventing the need for repair and in designing the vehicle to make repairs easier. Five mile per hour bumpers and flexible, "forgiving" fenders are examples. Most car lines have improved, but, among comparable models, U.S. cars have a lower average cost of repair than Japanese cars.

Insurance statistics show significant differences, some of which are quite dramatic. Part of the difference is related to size but design is a major factor.

## Styling

In the broadest sense of value to the owner, styling is an important factor. There are many remarkably attractive cars on the road and some others that are incredibly homely. The subject is too subjective, however, to try to name winners and losers.

## Corrosion Resistance

Extended protection against salt and the elements has been a long sought but elusive goal. Finally, however, in the past few years American manufacturers have done an outstanding job of designing corrosion protection into each new vehicle design. The use of coated steel, plastics, special sealants and coatings as well as a much better understanding of design for corrosion protection have led to the availability of cars unlikely to have panel penetration in severe climates for at least 5-10 years. I expect 10 year-panel penetration corrosion protection in future U.S. passenger cars and light trucks.

In my opinion the Japanese cars are significantly behind U.S. products in corrosion protection. This could be a time bomb because several years must pass before effects are seen by the consumer. Data on three years service requirements generally fail to show evidence of major corrosion problems.

## Drive Train Integrity

In the past 10-20 years we have almost forgotten about the engine, transmission, and final drive in modern cars. Not many years ago, owners expected to perform a "ring job" or "valve job" sometime during a car's life, but no more. The modern powertrain is a remarkable mechanism capable of 100,000 mile plus life with a minimum of maintenance. American car designers have emphasized this area for years because of the driving habits of the American consumer, who on the average, drives considerably farther than his European or Japanese counterpart.

I do not think the Japanese are yet producing cars of the extended durability potential of U.S. cars. I know of one advanced Japanese production engine that has been tested by one American manufacturer (a common practice). This engine has not been able to pass a severe, but routine, dynamometer durability test that essentially all American engines pass.

There is, however, one aspect of the drive train in which the Japanese excel. This arises from their attention to detail. Irritating minor malfunctions due to imperfectly installed engine drive train peripherals such as alternators, air cleaners, and the like require simple but exasperating repairs that occur all too often in the first year or two of owning a U.S. vehicle.

## Safety

Safety is a multidimensional factor that ranges from accident avoidance ability to crashworthiness. It may be the "sleeping dog" in the issue of Japanese vs. American passenger cars.

We have recently been through a phase of fuel efficiency patriotism. Maximum fuel economy was the major goal. The big car, if indeed one is still in the stable, is hidden from the neighbors' view and the newer, fuel efficient model occupies a position of prominence in the driveway.

Now we may be seeing the beginning of a new era in car ownership that I shall call "family first." Data are becoming available that show an alarming disparity between the safety of large and small cars. One recent study of fatal accidents with a very popular foreign make showed that a person was eight times as likely to be killed in that car than in an accident with any other vehicle.

It is clear that smaller cars are less safe than large cars. And not just when they get hit by large cars. Small cars are also less safe when they run into each other. However, NHTSA crash data (which I view with some reservations) show that American small cars fare considerably better than Japanese cars of similar size. Many factors are a part of these differences including overall design, efficient energy absorbing structures, good interior design, and rugged, penetration resistant body panels. The U.S. manufacturers have placed great emphasis here and have succeeded admirably in delivering excellent safety per pound of weight and at this writing appear to lead the Japanese competition.

Now to my "sleeping dog" theory. It may be patriotic to drive small cars, but I believe another motive is emerging that will place safety concerns ahead of energy for a significant portion of the driving public. "I want safety for my family," could be the rallying cry for millions of motorists and result in a shift in demand to somewhat larger vehicles and to those with better accident statistics.

The United States has an outstanding highway safety record. Japan's traffic fatality rate per 100 million vehicle miles was almost 62 percent higher than that in the United States in 1977, the most recent year available. This is an improvement since 1969, however, when the Japanese traffic fatality rate was over three and one half times the U.S. rate. The extent to which these fatality rate differences are related to average vehicle size is not known but could be significant. By far the safest place in the world to drive is on America's high-speed interstate highway system where the fatality rate is 1.5 per 100 million miles or less than half the U.S.

average of 3.4, which is in itself the lowest in the world for developed nations.

Other critical factors in safety include braking ability and handling. Handling we discussed earlier. Modern brake systems are excellent and there is little difference between U.S. and Japanese cars. Surprisingly, large cars often brake better, that is, stop in a shorter distance, than small cars.

## Conclusions Regarding Quality

From a technical standpoint, the passenger cars and trucks being produced in the United States, Japan, and in many other parts of the world are excellent, well-made machines that perform their intended functions with remarkable efficiency. In the past few years all cars have been improved dramatically and, except for model mix and fit and finish quality, U.S. vehicles are at least as good as Japanese products. However, a major task for U.S. manufacturers is to convey the importance and existence of "hidden" quality to technically untrained consumers.

U.S. management is now committed to matching Japanese perceived quality and has already begun to demonstrate its ability to do so. The quality problem facing U.S. automotive manufacturers is largely one of emphasis and timing—an abrupt increase in U.S. consumer attention to visible details. The U.S. public's sudden demand for visible quality creates a problem for U.S. manufacturers—not because they cannot create visible quality—but because the demand is sudden and comes on top of other pressures. Federal government product regulations absorb much of the financial and human resource base of American companies. U.S. automotive manufacturers have been forced to concentrate a large proportion of their manpower and capital on government regulations, while Japanese manufacturers have been free to concentrate on refining suddenly popular details.

Quality involves the entire industrial process from design to marketing. Quality, however defined, is a management responsibility. Any U.S. quality problem is not all the fault of the American worker; some of the best Japanese and German plants are in the United States. Although American workers are not the root cause of U.S. quality problems, systems to improve quality must take into account the U.S. worker as he is, not as he might be if born and raised in Japan.

We have heard an estimate that 1 in 20 U.S. production workers specializes in inspection and repair; we have not been shown proof that spreading these functions over all workers is a more efficient method. Quality control may appear to be less expensive when it is built in throughout the system, but its cost may be harder to measure.

The Japanese have succeeded in upgrading the quality of some of their products from a poor rating to excellent, but this does not prove that others cannot match or exceed their quality achievement or that the Japanese way is the only way. We must not assume that recent Japanese market successes are the result of everything the Japanese do, and therefore, that we should do exactly as they do. The Japanese culture gets a great deal of credit for Japanese quality, but it is the same culture that was once known primarily for "cheap toys"; when the need was perceived, the Japanese learned to produce quality products and so can we—whatever the definition of quality.

### Technical Education Needs

We agree with Science magazine that we must expand recognition of the enlarged dimension of science and technology in the affairs of the nation and the world. Our way of life relies heavily on science and engineering. The U.S. public should realize that technology is not just atomic bombs and nuclear power plants but also is warm houses and clean clothes and modern medicine and a car in every garage and supermarkets bulging with food. We need a better understanding of science and technology and more inputs from nonpolitical scientific advisers to reduce regulatory hysteria, decrease irrational and faddish public fears, and increase productivity.

Despite these pressing needs, the condition of science and engineering education in the United States has deteriorated seriously. Conspicuous American achievements, such as Nobel Prizes and space exploration, reflect the work of scientists and engineers from an earlier era. Japan and West Germany both graduate more engineers per capita than we do. In Japan, 20 percent of the undergraduate and 40 percent of master's degrees go to engineers. In the United States it is 5 percent for each level, and many U.S. graduates are foreign nationals who leave after graduation.

Universities are split into separate disciplines and departments and there is too little contact between them. Closer ties are needed not only between the social sciences, the physical sciences, and engineering, but also within these disciplines. For example, the two fields that will have the greatest impact on mechanical engineering in the 1980s are computers and materials—both of which are concentrated in other departments. Universities should make the teaching of engineering and science more relevant to industry. Basic research at the university level should be expanded and, in addition, entire new programs should be started in applied research, or engineering problem-solving research. By applied, or engineering research we do not mean product development—that is industry's job—but we refer to the need to tie the results of basic research into the manufacturing and product development processes. Industry—even in its basic research labs—puts multi-disciplinary teams to work toward a goal. Universities need to produce scientific specialists trained to work together.

A high priority should be placed on improving the understanding of science and engineering by company management and government and labor administrators. Minimal standards of technical literacy should be required of all who graduate from high school or college. Hundreds of thousands of Japanese workers have been trained in the mathematical and scientific principles underlying quality control. In the United States, only a few colleges offer a degree in the subject. In Japan, scientific instruction begins in the first grade. Science and mathematics are required and are two of the four major courses taught in the third through ninth grades. College-bound high-schoolers study probability and statistics and differential and integral calculus. Students in Russia face an intense mathematics and science curriculum. Algebra and geometry are taught in the sixth and seventh grades. Calculus is part of the high school curriculum and all students are required to complete four years of chemistry and five years of physics.

A Defense Department Science Board reported (among other grim findings):

1. A critical shortage of engineers, technicians, and skilled blue collar workers.
2. A shortage of 250,000 machinists over the next five years.
3. One engineering graduate in the United States to every six in the Soviet Union.
4. Skilled worker shortages are now 20 percent of needs and could be over 40 percent in ten years.
5. As a result of these shortages, many U.S. tooling and machining companies cannot meet demand—which is being sourced "off shore."

Engineering professors receive many requests from inventors who want endorsement for their wonderful new internal combustion engines that they believe to be twice as efficient as anything now in existence. Without exception, these inventions are not workable because they are based on a misunderstanding or ignorance of basic scientific principles. The tragic thing is that many of these inventors have spent thousands of hours and years of work and all their life's savings and they could have been headed off by an adequate understanding of high school physics.

The second edition of Modern English Usage by H. W. Fowler discussed "numeracy" as a requirement for nonscience graduates just as "literacy" is for scientists and engineers. Numeracy is defined as the ability to reason quantitatively and includes some understanding of scientific method, scientific achievements, and a rational understanding of scientific potentials and limitations. Much fun is made of the supposed illiteracy of engineers, but if we were truly as illiterate as many nonscience college graduates are ilnumerate, we would not be able to read or write and would sign our names with X's.

## Challenges to Both the U.S. and Japanese
## Automotive Industries

In less than 5 years, all U.S.-made passenger cars, except specialty models, will have the new, modern, front engine, front-wheel drive configuration. The largest Japanese manufacturers have just started on conversion to the new front-wheel drive technology. All major Japanese automotive manufacturers have at least one front-wheel drive car to offer, but the bulk of cars sold by the sales leaders, Toyota and Datsun, use a front engine, rear-wheel drive configuration. The capacity of the Japanese automotive industry is now about equal to that in the United States, so it faces a change-over task that, in many ways, is comparable to that in the United States.

Of course, the Japanese manufacturers will have the added advantage that their government will be helping them, but the challenge they face in converting to the vehicle of the future will prove almost as burdensome as in the United States.

A continuing threat to the successful turn-around of the U.S. automotive industry has been the instability and irrationality of Federal laws and regulations. Long-lead times force industry to start action today that will not be complete for 5 years; government policy sometimes seems to look no further than the two years to the next congressional election. We desperately need rational, long-term consistency of policy and laws affecting the automotive and energy industries. High levels of understanding and intelligent two-way communication between industry and government will be required.

In Japan the relations between labor and management, and between industry and government, are dominated by a long-term view of events. The United States also needs a consistent and positive national industrial policy. U.S. industry does not require an increase in government assistance: it very much needs a decline in government meddling.

Following is a list of some of the things that the U.S. government and industry can do to compete internationally and particularly with the Japanese:

1. Establish a stable, non-punitive government industrial policy that will encourage capital formation, development of productive manufacturing technology and outstanding new products.
2. Establish a joint industry-labor-government strategic analysis group to evaluate the total national impact of proposed legislation and regulation, international developments, technical trends, natural resource policies, etc.
3. Support long-range basic and applied or engineering research.
4. Strengthen technological understanding widely and in more than superficial depth.
5. Encourage and support greatly expanded interdisciplinary teaching and research at the university level.
6. Meet the Japanese (and German and others) quality challenge.
7. Encourage (and make legally feasible) much greater inter-company communication.
8. Reduce non-productive regulations.

The key, in summary, is to work together toward common, attainable goals.

# JAPANESE AUTOMOBILE MANAGEMENT PRACTICES

John Schnapp

## Three contrasts for your consideration:

American companies act as if they have shaped their managerial cultures around the belief that people are motivated primarily by money; Japanese companies have shaped their cultures much more around the belief that people are motivated primarily by the opportunity for personal growth and by contributing to creating a prestigious, winning organization.

American companies also believe that excellence of performance is stimulated by competition among individuals; Japanese companies believe, by and large, that success comes from encouraging individuals to contribute to group efforts, especially the effort of each individual's immediate work group.

Finally, American companies believe—or seem to believe, by their actions—that among all stakeholders, the interests of shareholders predominate; Japanese companies believe that the highest priority stakeholder is the employee "family," a "family" that includes both management and production workers together.

These three major contrasts in philosophy together, I think, account for most of the really significant differences in managerial practice at Japanese and American motor vehicle companies. There certainly is a barrier to belief here . . .

123

The Japanese philosophy may sound like an impossibly idealistic viewpoint especially when it is being manifested by organizations which—as competitors—reveal themselves to be so tough, tenacious, unyielding, intransigent and at times insensitive to some of the broader implications of their toughness. As a matter of fact, I think that the intransigent toughness demonstrated by Japanese automakers in the marketplace may be caused to some degree by this philosophic viewpoint. And this philosophy is also responsible for the lifetime employment system, for bottoms-up decision-making, for the importance of consensus and all of the other more familiar elements of Japanese-style management.

Cynicism about the humanistic foundation for the Japanese approach to management comes easily, especially easily to anyone who like most of us has spent his own working life in a different sort of business culture. I am sure that I started with the same sort of cynicism, but now, after three years as a witness, starting with intensive studies of the Japanese motor vehicle industry first for a European automaker and then for the U.S. Department of Transportation, and more recently through consulting projects for seven Japanese motor vehicle manufacturers and nine visits to Japan, my personal experience has overcome much of my own cynicism.

There are many inconsistencies in the Japanese style of management. Professor Yoshimatsu Aonuma of Keio University commented on this recently in The Wheel Extended. "There are many things classified as Japanese characteristics which are contradictory in nature," he wrote—"areas by no means easy for the Japanese themselves to understand. Foreigners, therefore, have an even harder time comprehending, and there are many examples of one face of an ultimately self-contradictory issue used to explain Japan overseas. The contents of such discussions thus tend to be shallow."

Superficiality is a very real risk to anyone like myself trying to fill 20 minutes for you with deep conceptual insight and wisdom about anything as complex as a wholly different managerial culture. I feel more comfortable in providing you, instead, with the more limited testimony of a witness, describing principally things I have personally experienced.

I would like to repeat the foundation beliefs of Japanese firms I mentioned at the beginning—belief in motivation by personal growth, belief in motivation by individual contribution rather than individual competition, belief in the primacy of the interests of the employee "family," a "family" encompassing managers and workers together. I want to run off for you an inventory of some of the managerial outcomes I've seen from this sort of philosophic foundation.

We all know about the lifetime employment system as practiced in large Japanese enterprises and about the tenure-related compensation system attached to it. Since a Japanese company is essentially "stuck" with its hiring choices, they are made extremely cautiously with a probing into personal attitudes, family structure, sense of responsibility, and other elements of character which would probably raise the temperature of the Equal Employment Opportunity Commission. (In fact, just a few days ago a Japanese friend was expressing to me his great concern that EEO ground-rules would prevent his firm from hiring attitudinally appropriate people in the United States.) But once you have a body of workers for their full working lifetime, what do you do with them? If you are a Japanese motor vehicle company, here are some of the things you do:

> You train them intensively, investing very considerable sums in this, so that their value to the firm—and to themselves—never stagnates.

> You let them run their own workplace with considerable autonomy when they are production workers, let them make decisions affecting work procedures and improvements.

> You encourage them to take problems and implement solutions through structures like the Quality Control circles which can caucus—and I have seen it—at any point during the workday and when meeting after hours, with compensation for those meetings. You get from this typically something like 18-20 productivity-related suggestions per worker per year.

You show trust in even larger ways; if you are Honda you let foremen in one plant be the principal designers of a new plant.

You try to keep the workplace from being boring and depressing; and even though the facades of most Japanese auto plants I have visited are disgracefully shabby by American standards the insides are quite another thing:  assembly workers typically do six to ten tasks, not one; almost no one works underneath the car during assembly but rather it is raised up and tilted to facilitate underneath work; really unpleasant and repetitious tasks are automated.

One leading figure in the Japanese motor vehicle industry has commented, "What I noticed at automobile factories in the United States was that the working environment was bad.  Decent people don't want to work at such places and as a result the quality of labor is poor.  The workshop should be a place where everybody finds joy in working and in earning his living.  An organization that enforces monotonous labor and deprives the worker or an opportunity to think may only work well for a while but is bound to get decayed in the long run."

When you have a philosophy in which the interests of the employeed "family" come first and in which motivation flows not so much from money as from contribution to creating and sustaining a prestigious, winning team, there are some equally interesting differences in management approach.

You don't play to the stock market; you don't allow managerial actions to be greatly influenced by the current whims and prejudices of analysts, institutional investors or the rest of the investment community apparatus. I have never heard a Japanese executive even mention in passing the price of his company's shares.  I would be surprised if anyone else in this room has either.

In bad times you keep your workers and may eliminate your dividends, not the reverse.

You have some surprising manifestations of democracy; there are virtually no private offices. As a visitor to a Japanese company you are brought to a quiet, serene, sometimes elegant meeting room and the walls of that room become a barrier between you and the work environment of the company; but if you get behind that wall, even as a temporary "member of the family," as I have been on a number of occasions, you find an atmosphere that looks as if it came straight out of a road company version of The Front Page, paperstrewn desks jammed together, people jammed together, and senior executives—people at levels comparable to executive vice presidents in American firms—jammed right in with their subordinates. And some of the presidential private offices I have visited are so spartan that they would offend a newly hired American college graduate, not to speak of a Harvard MBA.

Finally, you have great willingness of subordinates to press their ideas aggressively on their superiors, albeit with considerable show of respect, and you have also great reluctance on the part of superiors to reject such ideas. In fact, last week a Japanese friend who is a middle manager in a large automaker was commenting to me that if his chief should reject an idea in which he believed deeply, he would usually attempt to mobilize support among his own peers and they will together gang up on the boss.

This is, I recognize, a grab-bag of impressions on management style, but I can sum it up in another comment of the Japanese executive I quoted earlier. "It is wrong for executives to act like feudal lords and not know what is going on below them. What is more important in the process of democratization is for the upper people to come down. And that is where the sense of equality is found."

I would like to tell you two personal anecdotes which illustrate some of these points.

The first occurred two years ago when my colleagues at Harbridge House and I were engaged as consultants to a Japanese motor vehicle manufacturer during an intensive four-month effort to develop a plan for dealing with what was then—and still remains— the single most critical strategic issue faced by that company. Our work involved intensive two- to three-day progress review meetings at the company's head office every month. Most of the time these meetings were spent with an eight- to twelve-man team of middle managers, some of them quite young lower middle level managers, from the departments within the firm most deeply involved in the issues we were dealing with. (They characterized themselves as "working level staff" to distinguish themselves from their superiors, all directors and managing directors, whom they called "executive staff.") Then, on each visit, I would spend approximately two hours alone—no working level staff present—with the directors, the managing director, and the company president for a briefing by me to them.

My initial perception was that the leadership of our effort was coming from the executive level and that the working staff was simply doing the detailed dirty work. Gradually, through many small details, I began to perceive that quite the reverse was true. Policy was being formulated by the working level staff under an extremely permissive guidance from above. It began to dawn on me that my formal briefing meetings with the directors, some conversations at the desks of individual directors and evening social attentions from them were not much more than a courtesy to me and, because my role was a highly unusual one (Japanese firms not being prone to engage consultants, even round-eyed ones), they wanted to gauge for themselves the quality of my judgment to be certain that my influence would be a positive one on the working level staff. Bottoms-up decision-making.

The second anecdote. During 1980, one of the two Japanese motor vehicle manufacturers with an announced commitment to U.S. manufacture asked Harbridge House to present a series of advisory briefings and to participate in a series of discussions about the history, practice, and character of employee relations in the American motor vehicle industry, focusing especially on the opportunities for transferring elements of the Japanese employee relations system to the company's new U.S. plant. Once again this involved one afternoon spent with executive-level staff and day after day of highly detailed meetings with working-level staff, most of them attached to the client's U.S. project office.

As a means of preparing ourselves for these meetings we suggested that we spend several days visiting different representative plants of the company in Japan and chatting with small groups of junior foremen, senior foremen, and lower-level managers to acquire a more intensive view of the company's own employee relations system. I want to convey to you just one small and revealing detail from these conversations. It describes an example of the investment in people that prevails in the Japanese motor vehicle industry. By the time that young workers have eight to ten years of experience they may be considered for promotion to junior foreman. In this particular company, people considered as having the potential for promotion attend a training course called Advanced Skilled Workers Education. It is two months long, involving full-time off-the-job attendance. The teachers include both lecturers from outside the firm and executives from inside. The course provides particularly strong focus on quality control and supervisory techniques. Performance at the course becomes a major criterion for selection as a junior foreman. Once a man is actually selected he will then receive an additional four- to five-day intensive training course and will also be enrolled in a one-year correspondence course in problem solving designed by the Japanese Management Association. And then, periodically, small groups of junior and senior foremen will go off together for very intensive three-day special courses to keep their skills updated and constantly improved. Now in comparison, most of you know what foreman training amounts to in American motor vehicle firms; in one of the Big Three, I know it is nonexistent and in the others very nearly negligible in comparison with what I have just described.

This all is not to gloss over the fact that management in the Japanese motor vehicle industry faces some unusually severe challenges in the near-term future. One such challenge is multinationalism. With its tribal sense of clannishness, its scorn for the inhumanity it sees in foreign management philosophies—ours and Europe's—and its horror at slipshod, uncaring foreign workers—ours and Europe's—it will nevertheless be forced to live abroad. It will have to hire such managers and workers and to struggle to achieve with them the same high levels of quality and productivity improvement that characterize its activities in its home country. This will be a major test, in general. Nissan, Alfa-Romeo will be the epitome of such a test.

But there is another test that I think is of even greater magnitude. The structure of Japanese worker compensation—based upon tenure—is a tremendous engine of growth. Think about this. If a company is succeeding in a market that is growing rapidly, its workforce will be young, its average compensation levels low and its total costs equally low. We have estimated that labor cost rises between 5 and 7 percent with each one-year increase in the average age of a Japanese company's employee population. This cost advantage during growth is one of the reasons for the success of Japanese motor vehicle manufacturers in the world marketplace; it is also one of the reasons for their reluctance to manufacture offshore rather than in Japan and one of the reasons for their continual pressure for unit volume growth. But I think you can also see that once growth stops for a Japanese company—or a whole industry—the compensation systems works rapidly in reverse. The downside of the roller coaster can get very steep indeed.

In the next decade we at Harbridge House see very little growth in worldwide demand for motor vehicles and diminishing opportunities for the Japanese motor vehicle makers to increase their respective shares of the overall market, at least in the same simple ways they have in the past. (Of course, some of them are already demonstrating very creative ways of dealing with this challenge.) But if growth in the Japanese auto industry workforce stops and if that workforce begins to age with consequent rise in cost levels, economic disaster can be pushed back only by one thing—productivity gains. This will be an extremely difficult struggle. But I would also say in conclusion, that I have been strongly impressed at how widespread within these companies, right down to foreman level, there is a conceptual understanding of this problem and an equal dedication to overcoming it.

# RESPONSES OF CONFERENCE PANELISTS
## TO AUDIENCE QUESTIONS

Panelists for the afternoon question and answer session included David E. COLE, Director of the Office for the Study of Automotive Transportation, The University of Michigan; Robert E. COLE, Professor of Sociology and Director of the Center for Japanese Studies, The University of Michigan; John JACKSON, Professor of Law, The University of Michigan, and former General Counsel of the Office of the Special Trade Representative; Kaoru KOBAYASHI, Professor of the Institute of Business Administration and Consultant to Overseas Enterprises Institute, Japan; Ira C. MAGAZINER, President, Telesis, Inc.; the Honorable Donald W. RIEGLE, Jr., United States Senator from Michigan; and John SCHNAPP, Vice-President, Harbridge House.

Q: What do you as a Japanese specifically suggest that the United States do in resolving the import issue with Japan?

KOBAYASHI: Actually, I would like to direct my suggestion not to the United States government or the American people, but to the Japanese government and the Japanese people: we must be discreet in our dealings with the rest of the world, we must enlighten our self-interest, so that we are certain to pursue our best long-term opportunities. I think these import issues are very important for us, because if we are not able to have amicable and harmonious relations with the United States it is a great danger for Japan. Moreover, it might invite conflict and friction with other countries in the world, particularly with the Europeans. So I think now is the right time for us to use our discretion: on the auto trade issue, my personal opinion is that being discreet now should involve certain kinds of long-term voluntary Japanese restraints.

Q: Do you expect that the U.S. government will adopt some form of temporary trade restriction with Japan within a year?

RIEGLE: That's difficult to say, partly because the views of the new President aren't fully known. But if the analysis of the problem that Secretary Goldschmidt and his department have prepared is roughly accurate and our problems don't correct themselves in the next few months, I think the pressure for trade restraints will continue to build up. I expect that at some point, restraints will be instituted.

I believe the best restraints would result from voluntary negotiations. As a matter of fact, legislation I have introduced would create the clear legal right for the President to work out an orderly marketing agreement or a voluntary restraint agreement with Japan.

Q: What is the probable Japanese response to import restrictions: will they then try to compete with the larger U.S. cars— Mercury, Buick, Olds, and Cadillac, the cresta maxima type cars?

D. COLE: I think it's highly probable that they will. Some excellent larger, more luxurious vehicles are being sold in the Japanese home market that I expect to see here in the United States. Also a number of outstanding luxury or sporty type cars such as the the Datsun 280 Z car and the Mazda RX7 are already being sold here. The Japanese are certainly attracted to the higher profitability of these products.

Another aspect of this question is that because Japanese small cars are already very fuel-efficient, the Japanese manufacturers can easily market a sizeable number of less fuel-efficient vehicles in the mid-price or the mid-size range and still easily exceed the U.S. government's corporate average fuel economy standards.

Q: To what extent is the Japanese success in lowering costs the result of using temporary employees, primarily women, who do not enjoy the wages and benefits of full time employees, to handle peak production periods?

R. COLE: The percentage of temporary employees in the Japanese automobile industry has tended to decline, particularly in the parent firms, over the last 15 years, simply because the labor shortage has led industry to recruit them into permanent positions. The proportion of women workers in the auto industry in Japan is roughly 10 percent. (The employment of women has been restricted because of restrictions on night and shift work.)

But lower wage costs in Japan are also partly the result of structural differences between U.S. and Japanese industries. The total employment at Toyota Motor Company or Nissan Motor Company is about fifty to sixty thousand employees; the bulk of auto-industry employment is in fact concentrated in subcontracting firms. As a result, subcontractors to a considerable extent have served in the past to cushion the parent firms from the expense of providing high wages and benefits to employees whose work is essential to automobile production but who are not on the auto companies' payrolls.

D. COLE: Very often Japanese suppliers are really part of the same family—socially connected to the auto companies' management.

KOBAYASHI: Suppliers used to be called subcontractors, but the Japanese love euphemisms, so these people are usually called supporting industry people. It is also worthwhile emphasizing that the system of permanent employment affects only about a quarter of Japanese auto workers, although this proportion is increasing.

SCHNAPP: One further detail about the circles of suppliers that surround each of the major assemblers. The major members of the Toyota family of suppliers don't supply Nissan, and vice versa. For Japanese suppliers to subcontract work from their principal customer's major rival is very unusual.

Q: By closing the door partially to imported products, don't you think you are implicitly telling the domestic manufacturers that they don't have to worry about their inefficiencies, that "we will protect you"? Is this really effective in raising our competitive level over the long haul?

If the Japanese auto firms are building a superior product—providing the best value for the money—why shouldn't the citizens of the world be allowed to buy it?

RIEGLE: U.S. cars do not sell in Japan because the Japanese for many years had their market closed to foreign imports. As a result, no automaker outside of Japan even tried to build a car for the Japanese market. It has only been since 1978 that the Japanese opened their market to outsiders. But even this "opening" of the market doesn't really count because there are hidden traps and pitfalls, too numerous to mention here, in trying to establish a market in Japan.

There are many who say we ought to follow what Japan has done to become a world leader in small cars. I agree. We could start by giving our U.S. auto industry a three-year breathing spell by limiting Japanese imports to some reasonable level.

But that is not all. I have cited the need to defer all new government regulations for an indefinite time and to rescind certain other regulations that are taking money away from the retooling effort needed to build smaller, fuel-efficient cars. I have also sought a restructuring of our tax code so that distressed auto companies and suppliers can receive some major tax relief right now. I would also support other measures such as tax rebates to consumers.

While we may differ on how we got into the current dilemma, I would hope that we all can agree that we must rebuild our own auto industry back to a position of world preeminence. This will put hundreds of thousands of Americans back to work, revitalize our economy and maintain an industry that is important to our future.

Q: If Japan, Inc., is a myth, who does own the Japanese auto industry? To whom is the industry ultimately responsible? Who defines industrial policy, deciding how far to depart from free enterprise towards a government-controlled economy?

MAGAZINER: I think there is often a perception that if the government is allowed to get involved at all with planning and investment-decision making—or any such encroachment on what is thought of theoretically as the market's provenance—then immediately a fence has been jumped and the government will begin to dominate the national investment-decision-making process or institute centralized state planning. I think that kind of dogma is very misleading.

I think that in Japan, it is realized that 1) the market system is generally the best operator in most situations, but that 2) in some situations the government can play a role. The usual government activity to help accelerate market forces is in Japan supplemented by other less-public efforts: protecting both public and private interests by negotiating with industry on a whole series of questions relating to regulations, government funding, risky R & D, and so on. The Japanese government gives, in a sense, selective opinions to various industries about directions for industry development.

I have noticed that the audience today gives any comment which is critical of the government a round of applause. The government of this country has not pursued a conscious industrial policy and has promulgated a number of conflicting measures which have confused industry and which have certainly not encouraged development of our competitiveness. On the other hand, it is also true that some failures of business strategy at the management level, in this and other industries, have also had much to do with the problems various American corporations face today. Blame for our present difficulties should not be placed solely on either government or management.

What I think we need is to recognize that government does have a legitimate, though subservient, role to play, but that in order to be cost effective it does have to be a selective role. A general tax credit to industry, although that may in some cases be appropriate, is very costly; selective measures which will weed out cases where that money is not going to be spent well or is not even needed can often result in a better public good. Mistakes will be made, even in Japan: MITI has made mistakes, Japanese companies have made mistakes; but sometimes MITI has been right. The dynamic interaction between the two, I think, produces a very good policy most of the time, and that's all I would really suggest for us.

Q: All automobiles sold in the United States have the same regulatory requirements applied to them. Sometimes foreign firms have found it easier to comply, e.g., fuel economy. Sometimes U.S. firms have found it easier, e.g., safety. How is it possible then to say that compliance with regulation is the U.S. auto industry's biggest problem?

D. COLE: I don't believe that compliance with government regulations is the U.S. automotive industry's major problem, but rather only part of a larger problem. The most important source of difficulty has been the lack of a constructive relationship with government that will provide incentives and remove disincentives related to the production of modern automobiles. In Japan, on the contrary, an extraordinarily harmonious relationship exists between industry, government, and labor, which has led to strong incentives for the production and export of cars and light trucks. Regulations can be broadly classified as being applied to either the production process or to operation. Production regulations include OSHA standards and environment restrictions on plant effluent. They have become complex and enormously expensive to satisfy. While the

Japanese manufacturers face similar standards, their application has been more consistent and carefully thought-out from the standpoint of cost benefit.

In terms of regulations on performance (safety, emissions, fuel economy) small vehicles have a somewhat easier task in a number of areas, particularly fuel economy and emission control. Therefore, the typically smaller Japanese vehicles have a considerable advantage. The lower power requirements of the smaller vehicles result in less difficulty with emission control and obviously mean better fuel economy.

Q: How can top U.S. management convince middle management that quality is important and not just another fad to be pursued until auto sales again go up? What are some of the causes for the Japanese surge in quality? Was Dr. Deming part of it?

R. COLE: Top management convinces middle management that quality is important by putting systems in place to reward it, in other words, by putting their money where their mouth is. Obviously there are other kinds of rewards besides money—I don't mean to suggest that's not the case—but if you're serious about pushing quality then it must be monetarily rewarded.

With regard to the second question, I would make the following observation: clearly Dr. Deming's concepts of total quality control, as well as Drs. Juran and Feigenbaum's, were important influences on the Japanese approach to quality control. Dr. Deming's statistical approaches—particularly concerning assembly processes—are in our textbooks, but we don't seem to use them. I think what the Japanese did was to put together statistics with a system of management designed to promote quality.

Q: What corporate strategy accounts for the limited success of the U.S. auto industry in utilizing the mainstream of professional quality control?

R. COLE: There is no simple answer to this question. The failure to utilize the mainstream of professional quality control personnel reflects the relatively low priority assigned to achieving product quality compared to other parameters. It has not been uncommon to assign to quality control functions those who were deemed not capable of making it in line management. With the life and death priority now being assigned to improved quality, I anticipate that this will change. Similarly, we will see a greater importance attached to the use of statistical quality control methods now that the Japanese have demonstrated the extent to which they can be effectively used to upgrade product quality. This should enhance the clout of quality professionals.


Q: The auto industry knew the advantages of front engine/front-wheel drive cars for many years. Why did it take so long for the industry to give the public these advantages?

D. COLE: I don't believe that the advantages of the transverse front engine/front-wheel drive cars have become that important until recently. In fact, it was not until the fuel prices began to escalate rather dramatically that it became a cost effective technology in the U.S. market. Our studies have shown that the transverse front engine/front drive powered car will result in a 150 pound weight savings in a compact car and a 250 pound weight savings in a larger vehicle, which is important today but not in the early 1970s or earlier. Furthermore, only recently have technological advances been made that permitted the application of reasonable priced front-drive technology to somewhat larger vehicles. Early on only small subcompact cars were suitable for front drive because they did not have the basic structural requirements of larger vehicles. I might make an additional point here, and that is if we look at the Japanese automotive industry it is evident that the two major manufacturers, Nissan and Toyota, are in roughly the same position with regard to conversion to front drive technology as the U.S. manufacturers.

Front engine/front drive vehicles have faced continuing problems with 1) substantially higher drive-train costs particularly in the constant velocity universal joints required, 2) torque steer, 3) excessive tire wear, 4) traction with higher power to weight ratios, and 5) serviceability. Most of these problem areas are still important but they are offset today by the packaging advantages.

Q: What can automation do for American car quality?

R. COLE: Automation has an obviously important role to play in upgrading product quality. Nevertheless, we must not see the quality problem as one which simply can be met with a technological "fix." It is this instinctive reaction which put management into trouble with the workforce in the first place.

Q: Isn't Datsun's Nap-Z engine, which incorporates such advanced technology as fast burn and low friction, a sign of Japan's emergence as a leader in automotive technology?

D. COLE: It certainly is one sign. This is an outstanding new engine design. Although it doesn't represent what I would call inventive technology, it does represent an excellent application of known technology. The concept of a fast-burn, low-friction engine has been investigated by engineers all over the world, including some at our own laboratory. It promises benefits of reduced emissions and increased fuel economy. Clearly Nissan's production of this engine is a sign that Japan is emerging as a leader of automotive technology, but it is not evidence of total supremacy.

Q: Please comment on Japan's technology with respect to diesel engines (meeting the 1983 U.S. federal mandates) versus U.S. auto companies meeting these mandates.

D. COLE: Just as with the front-drive technology, the Japanese companies are in approximately the same position as the U.S. automotive manufacturers with respect to diesel engines. If they have any advantage it is probably due to the fact that their diesel engines will be powering somewhat smaller vehicles. Because of their lower power requirements small diesels have less difficulty meeting emission standards for pollutants such as particulates and nitrogen oxides. Both the Japanese and U.S. light duty diesel engines are excellent examples of advanced engineering at the present moment, and I suspect engines from both countries will be further improved in the next few years. In terms of advanced diesel technology for light duty vehicles I believe the Europeans are somewhat ahead of both the United States and Japan.

Q: Do you feel that current Japanese trade barriers are a minor, significant, or major factor in the current auto trade imbalance?

RIEGLE: Since U.S. auto manufacturers were shut out of that market for a considerable period, they cannot now suddenly penetrate it. I don't imagine that the Japanese market can become an important source of sales for American automobile products. There are many ways in which the Japanese could prevent that from happening, and one or more of those methods are likely to be used. And I admit that if I were Japanese, I would not want foreign automobiles to displace the domestic manufacturers'.

But the key question is the reverse: can the United States afford to let auto manufacturers of a single foreign country take 20 percent or more of our market over a continuing period? If Japanese sales figures are examined state by state, it is apparent that Japanese auto manufacturers have been pursuing a two-coast strategy. The proportion of the market now taken by the Japanese is much higher on the east and west coasts, so that in some parts of the country it is well over 20 percent.

SCHNAPP: I think the question of Japanese trade barriers is moot as far as the automotive market is concerned, because, very simply, through the long-standing protection of the Japanese domestic industry in its home market, the barriers to entry have become so costly to overcome that it would take an adventurous American or European firm ready to make a headlong effort in order to develop any sort of substantial penetration of the Japanese home market. These barriers today are not necessarily legal or even institutional ones; it's a financial barrier more than anything else.

RIEGLE: May I add that I was in Japan a few months ago, and asked (Ambassador and former Senator from Montana) Mike Mansfield to help an American auto dealer who is prepared to open an American automobile dealership in Tokyo. Even getting a single American entrepreneur into the ballgame over there was just out of the question financially.

Q: A major U.S. auto firm recently announced that they will work with a Japanese partner for the design of various components for a new mini-car to be produced in the United States in 1984. It is assumed that these components will be produced in Japan.

In your opinion do you believe that the reason for this decision was the greater expertise in Japan from a technical standpoint? If such actions continue, what will be the effect on the current domestic supplier base of these components?

D. COLE: There are several reasons why U.S. automotive firms are looking to Japan as a source of vehicle components. Several are particularly important. Perhaps the most important is lack of capital. When high quality components can be obtained from Japan at a reasonable cost, this reduces the capital investment required by the American manufacturers. Another reason is the high level of expertise available in Japan in several subsystem technologies. They have had considerable manufacturing experience, for example, with drive-train components for smaller vehicles. I expect that these actions will have a considerable impact on the domestic suppliers and I believe it emphasizes the importance for the suppliers to become international companies. Some of the lost business may be lost permanently unless domestic costs and quality can be improved. Furthermore, I think it is important to recognize that Japan is not the only off-shore source that the automotive manufacturers are considering. In a recent survey we conducted of U.S. automotive engineering executives, foreign sourcing is expected to grow in the future.

Q: A whole range of factors accounting for Japanese quality superiority have been suggested. Since everything can not be done at once, and not all Japanese practices are appropriate for the United States, what specific policies could U.S. auto firms follow to start closing the quality gap?

R. COLE: A) Work to improve the manufacturing-design interface with earlier and regularized input from manufacturing and quality control personnel into the design process. Such interaction should be based not only on formal meetings but on informal working relationships.

B) Explore opportunities for regularized information exchange with vendors so that they can be brought more into the total quality control activities of the auto firms.

C) Establish opportunities for hourly employees to regularly make input on quality-related matters. Work toward the creation of systems which allow all employees to take responsibility for the quality of their own work.

D) Examine existing reward systems and modify those that do not sufficiently reward the achievement of high quality.

Q: Shouldn't we leave the definition of quality to the consumer and market our products to their perceptions?

D. COLE: I think it would be ideal to leave the definition of quality to the consumer and the market if the consumer was capable of understanding the breadth of automotive technology. We have an obligation to help the consumer understand those factors that are part of the total value received in the product. These include such characteristics as structural integrity, corrosion resistance, crashworthiness, and maintenance requirements, that are not evident from a surface inspection of the vehicle but are truly a part of the value received by the customer. The notion that "beauty is only skin deep" applies to the automobile market as well as to the human race. Furthermore, since technology is moving so rapidly it is increasingly difficult for the consumer to rely on past history as a measure of current value.

Q: Hasn't the success of quality circles been overblown? If not, why have so many U.S. attempts at these kinds of activities failed?

R. COLE: There is indeed a tendency to exaggerate the impact of quality control circles, and there no doubt will be many failures in the future. Quality circles cannot carry the whole responsibility for improving quality. That is simply too heavy a load for the circles to bear considering they meet only one hour every week or so. It is important to keep in mind that in Japan the circles were the last link in a system of upgrading quality and diffusing quality consciousness throughout the firm. Those U.S. firms which are instituting circles without putting into place the prior building blocks will not have their expectations met.

Q: With a bottoms-up decision-making process, what functions are delegated to the executive level of management?

SCHNAPP: The Japanese sometimes use a word, mikoshi, for the functions of upper-level management. The term comes from a ritual involving the carrying of a portable shrine by a large number of people in a procession: one person, the mikoshi, stands up on top of the platform and exhorts everyone else to do good work. Some observers believe that the function of senior management in Japanese firms is like that of the mikoshi: to stand at the top and cheer everyone on to good efforts. That is something of an oversimplification, but it seems to me that such leadership serves as subtle guidance, and promotes an environment in which the bottoms-up system functions well.

KOBAYASHI: The function of top management in Japanese corporations is generally different from that in the United States. The image of the mikoshi, although exaggerated, does capture some of these differences. The first function of a Japanese senior executive is to be an effective and subtle persuader. If he has his own idea about how to innovate, how to make a plan change, he's not able to implement it just by issuing orders. He must go through another typical Japanese procedure for facilitating decision-making called nemawashi. Nemawashi literally means root-binding. If one wants to make some major change, like transplanting a tree, it is important to carefully dig out its roots, so that the tree can be pulled out "harmoniously" or with less difficulty or with the least cost. Top management in Japanese businesses is expected to be proficient at this process of carefully preparing for major policy changes; this can often be a difficult and frustrating role. And in addition they are expected to be good cheerleaders too.

Q: How do the Japanese and American auto firms compare with respect to the rewards they provide for employee suggestions?

R. COLE: The average award amount for suggestions at Toyota Motor Company in 1979 was around $5.00. This figure is fairly typical of the Japanese auto industry. At Toyota, there were only 819 awards of over $30.00, and only 86 awards of over $100.00. The maximum award at Toyota is about $200.00. By comparison, the average award at General Motors is about $100.00 and the maximum award is $10,000. Since the whole reward scale in the

Japanese auto industry is lower than that of the U.S. industry, it is difficult to assume simply that the U.S. auto firms are generating much better suggestions. Nevertheless, there is evidence that the Japanese encourage many minor suggestions, and as full participation by all employees as is possible. That is to say, the Japanese value highly the very act of making suggestions and assume that many small suggestions in the aggregate will produce larger returns for the firms. Estimated annual savings to Toyota from their suggestion system are put at a minimum of $250,000. This sum is contributed by the 40,500 Toyota employees who participate in the suggestion system (a 90 percent participation rate).

MICHIGAN PAPERS IN JAPANESE STUDIES

Printed and bound by CPI Group (UK) Ltd, Croydon, CR0 4YY

09/06/2025

14685672-0003